The
11%
Solution

7 Steps to
Make Your
Buck Go Bang!

by

Verena Somer

www.TheServiceAdvisors.com

The 11% Solution
First Edition
First published 2009
Copyright ©2009 by Verena Somer

Graphics by Bob Sharpe

ISBN 978-1467940092

verena@theSERVICEadvisors.com

Table of Contents

STEP 1

Repeat business is your hidden gold mine that makes life easier and business more fun. Don't just win a sale. Win a customer!

STEP 2

Discover what your customers really want - and how to give it to them.

STEP 3

Master the secret of recovering from disaster when things go wrong (and they will).

STEP 4

Uncover ways to improve your image and make the most of what you've got.

STEP 5

Know the powerful words that cost you nothing and mean everything.

STEP 6

How to hire top performing employees

STEP 7

Win the loyalty of your staff - it can be your most precious asset.

APPENDIX

Fans Speak Out

A Must Read!

Wow! I've read 100 or more business books, and I've never seen one this much fun to read. More than that, the 7 Steps in the book can help any business make more money.

Bob S. – Author, *How to Be a Network Marketing Millionaire*

A seminar in a book!

"Reading this book is like taking an entire seminar without leaving home. I highly recommend it."

Barbara B. – Consultant

Fun & Informative!

This book is easy to read and chock full of ideas on how to retain and expand your customer base. Verena's sense of humor adds just enough levity to keep you engrossed. Follow her advice and your business can't help but grow. I recommend it highly.

Tom S. - Real Estate Developer

The 11% Solution

Thanks for the Info!

Verena, is a great resource. We experienced a significant improvement after her trainings. Check out her book.

Desiree A. – Business Owner

Sleep With It!

Easy read - Anybody who is serious about his/her business should sleep with it under his pillow for a quick nightly reference! I recommend it!

Beth C. - Executive Director

Read it NOW!

I've been in business for 40 years and could have used the information in this book a long time ago. If you were to learn just a few simple techniques outlined in "11%" you would be keeping more of your customers.

Smitty - Business Owner

Wonderful Resource!

In six months, we grew our business by 30%! We've implemented priceless tools that have enabled us to thrive when other businesses continue to falter. "Congrats Verena! You are a wonderful resource to business owners everywhere."

Giancarlo L. – Chiropractor

Award Winner!

After 6 months with The Service Advisors, we were awarded "The Best Personal Trainers" of the San Gabriel Valley.

Lorraine S. - Business Owner

Inspiring!

A HUGE THANK YOU to the Service Advisors. Your insight to how people think and react has been the inspiration for our website re-design. Verena rocks.

Kevin S. - Business Owner

The 11% Solution

Works Like Magic!

Verena gave me the 6 key words that work like magic when I need to win people over...

Kathryn R. - Business Owner

Grow Membership!

In 2007 we lost 77 members. The Service Advisors helped us reduce that number to ZERO.

Beth C. - Executive Director, Chamber of Commerce

The Best!

Verena's book is one of the best books ever written on Customer Service and keeping your customers happy.

Barbara W. - Executive

Introduction

The Cost of Poor Service

Quality customer service seals the deal for repeat purchases, and it is the most cost effective growth source for your business. Yet, according to marketing strategist Michael Hepworth, owner of the Results Exchange, most businesses can lose 11% of their revenue due to unhappy customers.

Think about it – what does that 11% number mean to you? If you're OK with leaving 11% "on the table", then everything is peachy keen, and you can stop right now. You don't need to waste your time in reading what I have to say.

But, if you're the kind of business owner that is always looking for "no cost" ideas to help your business grow, then read on. . .

There are very few companies (approximately 8%) that take a broad view of the customer experience. These elite firms focus beyond just improving products and services. They surprise and delight their customers, because they make them feel important. These customers, in turn, generate thousands of dollars worth of word of mouth advertising.

Okay, okay, I get it! Customer Service is serious business! And, the great thing is, it costs you exactly

The 11% Solution

nothing to be an 11% winner! Why? Because it's all behavioral-based – you can choose how you want to act. And, that costs nothing! You don't have to go to the store and spend money on trinkets, or think up some cute and clever campaign slogan to grow your business. But, there is a cost to poor service.

Which customer can you afford to lose?

I know you've got someone in mind. Is it the one that complains all the time? Or the one you can never seem to make happy? Or maybe it's the silent saboteur, the one who had a bad experience and just walks away – never to return – but likely to share their experience with friends and family at least 15 times a day.

Your customers have more POWER now than they've ever had before. If you think I'm kidding, just Google *"talking about customer service"* or a similar phrase. You'll discover pages of links to customer service stories, both good and bad. They name names and discuss experiences, and you are powerless to change the opinion once it's on "the Net".

Let me give you an example of how Viral a bad customer service experience can be.

A gentleman was hospitalized and left in a skimpy gown, on a gurney, in a hallway for hours!

12

Introduction

According to his VIDEO, (yes, I said video!) all staff members just passed him by. No one offered him a blanket or asked what they could do to make him more comfortable.

And the kicker is this . . . the poor service happened 15 years ago. But, he states very clearly, that he is, still today, more than happy to share his story with anyone who will listen!!!

How many people do you think he influenced with his story? Pick a number – or better yet – let's just arbitrarily say that he shared his story with thousands of people who saw this training video.

Talk about Viral! And this occurred long before the advent of You Tube, the Internet, Facebook or Twitter!

I'm sure we can all agree - -some customers are just a pain in the "you know what!" So why not just cut them loose? Your life would be a lot less stressful if you never saw them again, so why do your absolute utmost to keep EVERY customer? BECAUSE. . .

It costs 6 times more to gain a new customer than it does to keep one.

The 11% Solution

Here's an interesting factoid:

San Francisco, November 17, 2009

According to a new international survey of consumers sponsored by Genesys Telecommunications Laboratories, the cost of poor customer service in 16 major industrialized economies causes businesses to lose:

$338.5 billion per year in lost business

The average value of each lost relationship across all countries surveyed is:

$243 per year.

(YIKES! And there's more . . .)

Consumers feel the most significant causes of poor service are:

- Being trapped in automated self-service
- Being forced to wait too long for service
- Repeating themselves
- Representatives that lack the skills to answer their inquiry

Those are some big numbers, so it may be a challenge to relate them to you - the average business owner. But, here's another way to look at it.

Did you know that 11% of your profit may be lost each year due to unhappy customers?

Consider this:

Suppose you have 500 customers that brought you $100,000 net profit. On average, that means you can lose $11,000 (11%) due to poor customer service.

Do you really want to lose $11,000 next year? Because, if your service is lacking, 11% of your customers won't be back, and you'll have to replace them just to stay even.

How much will it cost to replace the 55 customers you lost, versus the cost of keeping them? Most experts agree that it costs 6 times more to acquire a new customer than it does to keep an existing one.

So, if it costs you $100 in marketing and advertising costs to get a new customer, that's $5500 that you could spend somewhere else.

And, remember, if you don't replace them, you're out $11,000.

New Car Anyone?

Now, tell me, is it really worth it to let that annoying customer walk away? No matter how "wrong" they are, or how badly they tick you off? Why not recapture the 11% who walk away – never to return?

"Recapturing" a customer, or regaining a customer's good will – even when you think they've created the problem – may require some "mea culpa's."

For example, I learned a long time ago to bury my ego - it has no business in your place of business. When I buried my ego, and learned how to take responsibility for the customer experience, I began to learn how to keep my customers and recapture lost profits.

And, as a bonus, I get enormous satisfaction from turning the unhappy customer into one that feels truly cared about.

I find it frustrating to know that I might be "leaving money on the table. Don't you?" Wouldn't you like to cut your advertising budget in half and grow your bottom line?

Just what can you do to keep those customers (and that $11,000)?

Introduction

Well, it's no secret - customers throughout the world value:

1) Time
2) Quality–Product Guarantee, and
3) Service *that makes them feel important.*

When they don't feel that they've gotten your time, a quality product or received service that makes them feel important, they're likely to become unhappy.

Losing 11% of your net worth to unhappy customers is a problem.

You can create Time, Quality & Service – and do it for NO COST. And it's so easy. . .you can get started today! The minute you turn the handle on your office door!

Remember - You don't have to lose your hard-earned money to a customer's perception of poor customer service.

I've got the 11% Solution!

Read the 7 Steps in the following chapters and learn exactly what you can do to give your customers what they value (Time, Quality & Service), and do it the NO COST way.

Introduction

We all know that successful companies today are the ones that revolve their business around their customers. But, can you be successful and still have room for improvement?

Always.

Everything is in the details. How we look, how our workplace looks, how we speak, what we say, even asking your customers what they prefer – it all says to them that you care about their initial experience, and you want them to come back.

Now, you're probably saying to yourself that customer service is the easiest aspect of your operation to tackle, right? But, it probably gets the least attention. (I could be wrong, but I'm guessing that your day may be a little pre-occupied with meeting payroll and coordinating multiple due dates, etc.)

So if it's so easy, why is it that two thirds of customers complain they aren't satisfied with the response to their complaint, and 90% of that group won't come back for the repeat sale. Not because of the product, but because of the service!

The 11% Solution

Given the fact that it costs six times more to get a new customer than retain an existing one, that statistic should matter to you. So, it might just be worth it to take a look at your customer service, and make some tweaks that will take your customers from "good" to "super loyal" – and reclaim that 11%.

After all, don't you want your customers to talk about you and tell others how great you are? Word of Mouth is the least expensive way to advertise. And, now, you've just made your buck go BANG!

So, what makes this book different than all the other books and seminars on customer service?

Good question. If you own a business, work for a business owner, or have any kind of contact with another human being, you simply don't have time to sift thru 269 pages for that one "nugget" of information that's a perfect fit for you and your business. Nor do you have an extra eight hours in your day to attend that $499 seminar!

If you do have the time & the money to attend the latest craze, I'll bet you dollars to donuts that you'll come home, put your notebook with the DVD and all the notes on the shelf, and never look at it again! (I must admit, I have a few notebooks on my shelf – so you're not alone!)

I don't know about you, but my eyes glaze over when I get too many words on a page, and my mind tends to "wander" if the paragraph or chapter goes on too long. If I read before I go to bed, I'm good for about 3 pages, and then I have to close one eye and squint with the other to see anything clearly!

Introduction Part Deux

So, considering that you might be a lot like me, I've developed the "11 % Solution" so it's easy to read (lots of white space), and only takes 15 minutes per chapter. (That, I can do!)

This guidebook has graphs and pictures of tools that illustrate the tried and true techniques and strategies that have served me well over the years. I guarantee that you'll find something regarding your service delivery that will either be a new idea, or give you an "aha" moment.

Don't be like me. I've made countless errors on the path to achieving the perfect balance between customers, staff, and satisfaction. I think back on how I handled certain situations, and to tell you the truth, I find my behavior embarrassing.

Just think of all the people I handled poorly - all the customers that I must have "put off" as a direct result of my poor service. I was an "11% loser", but no more.

I doubt that you have 25 years to invest in the kind of trial and error that I went through, but if you have 15 minutes, I can make this easy for you. (And, believe me, in 25 years, I've had a lot of "trial and error!"

Do it the right way. Take advantage of my mistakes, and in the process, save yourself some time and energy (and cash)! Let someone else (like me) sift through hours of seminars and pages of resources to bring you the best tips and most successful strategies – that guarantee a satisfied customer, a productive work environment, and a happy staff.

The 11% Solution

The "7 Steps" outlined in this book, are my constant companion. I know they work, because not only have they led me to receive several leadership awards from staff and colleagues, but I've used them to turn around more than one unhappy customer.

Using the "7 Steps", I've created many customers and employees who are my best advertisement and "super-loyal", word of mouth fans!

Today, it's not enough to say that focusing on your customers is important to your organization. You must be clear about what good service "looks like."

I can tell you what good service looks like. Better, yet, I can tell you what it "feels like."

Good customer service "feels like" every transaction, every moment a customer spends with you and your staff, is rewarding and valuable, and brings a smile to his/her face.

It's got a name, and it's called a "culture of service", and it encompasses the "experience", from the website to the phone to the parking lot to the waiting room, to the final delivery of your product or service.

But, "Building a Service Culture" sounds intimidating, and, perhaps, overwhelming. And, because I know your time is valuable, I give you a solution. In just 15 minutes, you can read one step of the 11% Solution, and your mind will be racing with ideas that you can't wait to implement.

Introduction Part Deux

I guarantee that when you follow just one of the recommendations in the 11% Solution, you will make it very clear to everyone who works with you that you consider service a priority.

Because of your focus on service, your staff, your colleagues and your customers will know exactly what good service "looks like," and you'll be one step closer to making your buck go BANG!!

It doesn't matter which step you start with; they work either independently or in harmony with one another. So, you can do one step, or all 7 Steps, in any order, and at any time that feels right to you.

But, before you get started, I do have one pointer.

Everyone needs to know if, and how much, success you're having with any of the 7 Steps. It's just like the thermometer used to track your local library's fundraising efforts. The library very visibly displays a thermometer that is updated regularly to reflect "dollars donated", keeping everyone in a giving mood, and offering recognition to their donors. Every time we drive by the library, we look to see how close they are to reaching their goal!

And, you should do the same thing.

Keep you and your staff in the mood to build your service culture by sharing your results often. It's not only fun to watch your progress, but watching that thermometer grow is critical to the success of any process. Enthusiasm for your efforts will stay strong, only if you communicate the results frequently.

The 11% Solution

So, together, you and your staff pick a measurement that all of you can agree on. It may be "dollars sold in a month", or "the number of missed due dates." I have a friend who wants to increase the number of piano lessons she teaches each week. She currently gives 5 lessons, and wants to grow to 20. She's already picked her measurement, and looks forward to reaching her goal.

Whatever you choose, it doesn't have to be super-scientific. Just pick a measurement and talk about it frequently. You'll be pleasantly surprised that spending a little time to focus on service has widespread, and positive, implications on your entire operation.

Before I go further, let me take a brief moment to pause and acknowledge an important matter. As you read on, you'll undoubtedly recognize some of the customer service strategies listed in this 11% Solution that you already do on a daily or weekly basis.

Congrats! It gives me great pleasure to recognize your achievements and validate your success. In fact, I'd love to hear more about what works for you. Just go to my Blog at www.theserviceadvisors.com/blog/ and share your customer service "tips" with other business owners looking to grow their business with no cost solutions.

Now, if you're curious about how to find an easy, no cost solution, to start that word of mouth engine – what are you waiting for? You're a business owner! You know how to make things happen! Read *The 11% Solution: 7 Steps to Make Your Buck Go Bang* and start to build your service culture one step at a time!

Introduction Part Deux

Remember, there is a significant prize to be gained by focusing on improving customer service. Start your service culture "campaign" today. *The 11% Solution* is the perfect road map to help you get started.

STEP 1

Check Your Engine

Our life is frittered away by detail. Simplify, simplify."

Henry David Thoreau

I call this step "Check Your Engine," because I'm a Service Advisor, and if you look up "Service Advisors" on Google, you'll find me, plus a boat load of automotive technicians!

The 11% Solution

Now I know nothing about how to help you with your BMW or your Honda, but I do know a lot about customer satisfaction, building the experience, creating a "Service Culture", and, simply, what it takes to get you the repeat sale.

In my 25 years in the service industry, I've seen "customer service" morph from "smile when you answer the phone" to "customer relationship management." It's grown from lessons about answering the telephone in 3 rings into how to develop a "Service Culture" that encompasses the customer "experience" from A – Z.

As you probably know, Service is so much more than picking up the phone in 3 rings, so before we get started on building your Service Culture, let me help you do a quick "tune-up," add a quart of oil and change the filter.

Before we get started on the other 6 Steps in this guidebook, take a look at a few of these best practices that I've carried over from job to job in the service industry. They are simple, easy to implement and useful, and a great way to "Check Your Engine."

And, don't let their simplicity fool you. They are powerful, effective, time-saving strategies. (In fact, I use them over and over again, because they are so darned effective!)

I also promise to reveal the big Leadership secret. So keep on reading. . .

Step 1 – Check Your Engine

Pay & Educate

"Pay & Educate" is a process that can de-escalate and de-fuse a problem, making you appear to be naturally helpful and concerned, and all the while, you're building trusting relationships with your customers. It's also a great role-modeling technique, and a sure-fired way to create "word of mouth." Here's how it goes:

1. Apologize for any confusion

2. Gently educate the customer on the product or policy and, again, apologize for the confusion (avoid using the words "should have," or "our policy is.")

3. Give the customer the product or service at a reduced rate, refund their money, give them a generous discount, or offer their next visit at no charge. This is the right way to "make nice" for the inconvenience they've experienced.

4. Thank the customer for bringing the problem to your attention and allowing you to fix it.

Tip: I offer "words to avoid", because in the corporate world, I used to prepare reports on complaint data. The largest number of complaints was generated because the customer was told *"It's not our policy to. . ."*

Back to the point. . .

The 11% Solution

This "Pay & Educate" process was used on me by my local grocery store the other day, and I just had to smile, because they followed the steps so perfectly. Here's what happened:

I ran out of shampoo, but when I went to the store to buy more, I picked up a bottle of conditioner by mistake. I went back to the store to return it, and waited in line at customer service. (Oh, did I mention that I no longer had the receipt).

The customer service line wasn't moving, and I was getting just a little bit antsy. So I decided to go to the shampoo aisle, and make the exchange myself. (My bad!)

I knew I had misbehaved by doing this exchange without "checking in", so feeling guilty, I decided to stop again at customer service on my way out.

The clerk listened patiently to my story and said,

"No problem. So sorry the line was long. But, we do need to report the exchanged item, so next time, just stop by here before making any exchange on your own. Have a nice day and thank you for shopping at Albertson's."

OK, that felt good, but now was I just supposed to walk out of the store with a bottle of shampoo in my hand. Was I going to set off an alarm?

Step 1 – Check Your Engine

She smiled reassuringly, and advised me that all was OK.

She could have argued with me, told me that I "should have" followed procedure or the "company policy is to. . . ", or sent me go back to the shampoo aisle and retrieve my exchange, but she didn't do any of that.

Instead, she used the "Pay & Educate" process – gently educating me on how to make the process work better for me the next time I had to make an exchange. And, she saved me the embarrassment of NOT pointing out my bad behavior! The "Pay & Educate" process helped me "save face", and made me feel alright about making a mistake..

People very much appreciate when you help them "save face." They'll talk about your great service skills, while telling the story to their friends and family. In fact, now I'm telling my story to a bunch of complete strangers! Good "word of mouth" advertising for Albertson's!

So, instead of popping me on the nose like a naughty puppy, which is humiliating and has a high probability of making the problem worse (it doesn't work for puppies either!), "pay & educate" is a process that is very simple. It's a professional way of solving a problem, showing respect, and creating a super-loyal customer that returns again, and again!

Thanks Albertson's!

The 11% Solution

The Huddle

Otherwise known as the staff meeting. However, if you call it a staff meeting, it implies a certain sense of formality. On the other hand, "The Huddle" is mainly an informal way to gather information and a great way to start off the day.

"The Huddle" gives everyone a sense of well-being and enthusiasm for tackling the day. "The Huddle" works well if you have one employee or 20. It can happen daily, or once a week.

"The Huddle" gives staff an opportunity to volunteer to handle new assignments and voice their opinions on how they think the day should be organized.

This "forum" of openness and safety, creates an environment that encourages your staff to speak up. It gives them the opportunity to share their ideas, and to influence operations. "The Huddle" also affords you an opportunity to "shine" as a leader that not only respects and values input, but is also willing to listen to others.

For example, I've worked with clients that had non-stop customer interactions, with the phones ringing off the hook the minute the doors opened for business. Almost daily, this client had at least one staff person who was either absent, had to leave early, or was unable to perform their regular duties.

The client started having Huddles every morning to share information about who was available, who had

Step 1 – Check Your Engine

called in sick at the last minute, who was stuck on the freeway, etc.

As a result, "The Huddle" eliminated confusion by quickly assessing the needs of the day, gave everyone an opportunity to rapidly re-assign daily tasks (or volunteer to take on additional responsibility), and allowed the manager to delegate coverage for any gaps in operations.

The staff also used "The Huddle" to share information about equipment issues, review the daily production board, and get everyone involved in brainstorming solutions to last minute problems. It's also a great way to offer a compliment to someone for something.

If an individual missed "The Huddle", they missed out on getting information that was critical to making the day go smoothly. As a result, this "uninformed" state is very likely to negatively affect the overall performance the team – a sure-fired way of inviting unwanted peer pressure.

Staff and manager began to look forward to "Checking the Engine" via the daily Huddle.

After a couple of months of consistently holding a daily, morning discussions, the staff realized the manager was serious about "The Huddle." They began to acknowledge the routine by getting their coffee early and starting to assemble for the morning's Huddle - without being asked. They also clearly enjoyed the recognition the manager gave to them daily, as a result of providing smoother, hassle-free service to their customers.

The 11% Solution

This, in turn, had a positive, spill-over effect on all other aspects of service.

The unexpected bonus was that lateness issues and absenteeism decreased. "The Huddle" was a simple and easy way to "Check Your Engine," and get everyone involved in starting the day off right.

As their customer satisfaction scores increased, "The Huddle" quickly became a standard component of my client's "service culture."

Call Backs

This is my absolute, all-time favorite, and a simple, simple way to "Check Your Engine." The rewards are so immediate and gratifying - plus revenue-generating - that I can't imagine not doing call-backs.

But, why should YOU do call-backs? Because, call- backs are THE step that creates a memorable customer experience. Customers love getting a call to ask how they're doing. Don't try to sell them on anything, don't try to book the next appointment, just ask how is the product or service is working out for them. Consider this:

Even in a negative economy, customer experience is a high priority for consumers, with 60% often or always paying more for a better experience.1

And, call-backs give the customer an invitation to express their opinion. If they happen to express a negative or dissatisfied opinion, then you have an opportunity to fix the problem.

Customers who get their issue resolved tell about 4 to 6 people about their experience[2]

More "Word of Mouth" = more "Ka-ching!"

There are 3 major secrets to conducting a successful call-back campaign, and I'm going to share them with you, now.

(1) The List

As with so much of this "service" stuff, you've got to have a list. If you don't have a "contacts" list, hopefully, you can fulfill this requirement by printing out a list of "recent transactions" from your customer database.

---

[1] Harris Interactive, Customer Experience Impact Report
[2] White House Office of Consumer Affairs, Washington, DC

The 11% Solution

(2) Timing is everything

Once you've printed a list of your recent transactions, be mindful of the timing between the close of the transaction and the phone call.

For example, calling too soon doesn't allow the customer time to fully experience the product or service, and if there is an issue, calling too late allows the customer time to fume and tell a million other people about the problem.

(3) No agenda

My recommendation is to call the customer, and ask about something personal that you learned via their recent interaction with you. For example, how was that event they were planning to attend back East, or how was their vacation, or their family reunion?

This is why you want to take notes and personalize their file – just jot a quick note on their sales slip – in order to personalize your follow-up conversation. This is what I mean when you call back "with no agenda." There is no discussion regarding their next purchase. If you impress them with the call back, they will naturally return to you the next time they're ready to buy.

Step 1 – Check Your Engine

Why do call-backs? Four reasons:

1. Staying in touch with the customer is always a "good thing." (They'll be pleasantly surprised at your phone call, and be more likely to tell their friends about it.)

2. Calling to ask about the customer's event, or a vacation, (maybe they're getting a new puppy or putting in a pool for their kids, etc.) shows that you were listening, and you care about more than just "making the sale."

3. Providing the customer a timely opportunity to comment on the product or service shows you're interested in making it right and not afraid to talk to them about their satisfaction (or possibly, dissatisfaction). Most importantly, this call-back conversation gives you an opportunity to "fix" an issue before it becomes a complaint.

4. Collecting on an outstanding payment, or getting a new order is always a very real possibility during a call-back phone call. (And who doesn't want more business and more money!)

For example, I ran into a business owner the other day, who opened a medical supply store right before the economy tanked. Two and a half years later, he's still in

The 11% Solution

business, and doing better than ever! What made him so recession-proof?

Since I'm always gathering best practices, I asked him about his service policies. What activity(ies) did he attribute to his success?

Call-backs. He swears by them. It's part of his daily routine to always call back the customer and ask how they're doing, and "is there anything he can do to help."

In fact, he has a system set up to strategically time his calls. The first is in 3 days, the next in 2 weeks, and the third

in 1 month – always mindful to tell the client, up-front, that he will be calling them in a few days just to check up on them, and to see how they're doing.

You can tell from just talking to him, that he's a really concerned and caring guy, but he attributes the majority of his success to this one process.

Second example: I asked a business-owner friend of mine to help to "test" the call-back process. (Was it as good as I thought?)

She made 8 call-backs from her list of transactions that closed in the previous week. Five of those eight phone calls resulted in new orders or payments of outstanding invoices. That's a success rate of over 60%!

Step 1 – Check Your Engine

So, if you're not doing call-backs, add some oil to your engine, and start doing them today. It's worth giving it a try, and your customers will love you for it!

And Now. . . . (drum roll, please)

The Big Leadership Secret

Revealed!

■ ■ ■ ■ ■

Call it what you want – "Walk the Talk", "Accountability", "Do What you Say You Will" – the big Leadership secret is . . .

"Follow-thru"

and it's the most important Leadership behavior that you'll ever adopt.

The 11% Solution

Let me ask you a question - When you introduce some of these new service initiatives to your staff, are you worried that they'll stare at you like bumps on a log? Or will they politely listen, and then turn around and do their own thing?

Do you ever get concerned that you'll spend your time implementing some new initiative and by next year (or next month!), it will be only a memory? Will it have fallen by the wayside like so many other good ideas?

Stop wasting precious time and money on an initiative only to have it turn out to become the next "flavor of the month." You'll get discouraged and your staff will become jaded.

Whatever new action you choose, give it some "legs" – make it have some lasting power. Here's how:

Every initiative requires execution. And a critical part of the execution plan is "Follow-Thru." Unfortunately, this is where the rubber meets the road, and I know that you're often so burnt out from multi-tasking and juggling your business and personal life, that this step of the process doesn't get the attention it needs.

We're here to make money, not waste money. And, if there isn't a "Follow-Thru" plan, get ready to throw good money after bad. Here are some tips that will give your initiative traction and help you execute the "Follow-Thru."

Step 1 – Check Your Engine

Implement one initiative at a time

Don't bite off more than you can chew. Pick a step that you can really get behind and then see it thru. Ask how it's going every day. Then, staff will see that you take this initiative seriously.

Remember, It takes 8 weeks for a new process to become habit. Resist implementing a new process until you've mastered the previous one.

Delegate

You don't have to implement any initiative alone – in fact, it is preferable that you don't. Use another person on your staff to be the "lead" for at least one piece of the process. Let them participate in the training of others and introduce them to staff as your "go to" person for any questions or concerns.

Communicate Often

Use everything at your disposal – e-mail, fax, phone, and staff meetings – whatever is convenient for you - to communicate the status of your initiative to the staff.

My favorite communication venue is a weekly staff meeting – but, that's not always possible. So do whatever it takes. Even if it's to say, "How's it going?"

The 11% Solution

Utilize your "lead person" to help you communicate frequently.

Recognize Frequently

This is a chapter unto itself, but deserves mention as a "Leadership Secret."

If you want people to continue to be enthusiastic about a new initiative, you MUST use recognition to get them to repeat the behaviors that you find desirable. A simple "Thank You" will do the trick. A hand-written note is even better.

Wouldn't you like your staff to do anything in the world for you? Read "Share the Love" and find out how to "rock" recognition.

Then, make it a point to thank a person every day for something!

I keep a copy of these Leadership Behaviors taped to the inside cover of my calendar.

Step 1 – Check Your Engine
LEADERSHIP BEHAVIORS

There is a link between a strong service culture and high levels of customer satisfaction. A leader concerned abut the customer is:

- **PASSIONATE**
    - o Always go out of your way to meet the customer's needs
- **COMMUNICATES CLEAR EXPECTATIONS**
    - o Holds staff meetings that have "service" on every agenda.
- **LISTENS AND ACTS ON STAFF SUGGESTIONS**
    - o Include your staff in the decision making process – implement some of their ideas.
- **OBTAINS RESOURCES**
    - o Removes barriers to good service – Do your best to get the staff what they need.
- **RECOGNIZES SOMEONE EVERY DAY**
    - o Frequency is the key.
- **DEMONSTRATES EMPATHY**
    - o Show that you care – listen more – speak less
- **ROLE MODELS**
    - o Do the right thing – walk the talk – keep your promises.

Figure 1.0 – Leadership Behaviors

My all time, super duper, favorite thing - is to the "Push the HELP button." Here's how:

4 Words

That Will Change Your LIFE

"I need your help."

These four little words have an amazing affect on business associates, friends and family! They've made a huge difference in my life, and they will in yours, too.

Now, I realize that this is a difficult task for some business owners. For example, I mentioned it to a friend the other day, and asking for help just doesn't feel right to her. She's started up her business for 30 years ago, all by herself, and didn't have any help from anyone. And she's very successful. So, to her, asking for help is a sign of weakness.

Au contraire! (That's French for "Everyone loves being "tapped" to HELP their boss.")

Not only will it make a HUGE difference with your staff, but you've got to try this on your friends and family. That's it – I don't need to say a lot more about it. It's one of those "Check Your Engine" things that's so simple, you may think it won't work!

But, if you don't try it, you'll never know. . . .

STEP 2

Measure for Success

"Before we build a better mousetrap, we need to find out if there are any mice out there."

--Yogi Berra

How much do you spend on coupons, fliers, ads in magazines, newspapers and radio? If you have a budget for advertising, wouldn't you like to cut it in half? Or, at least, make your buck go BANG!

Not interested? Then you must be one of those business owners who have limitless funds or you're satisfied with just coasting along or. . .

The 11% Solution

Maybe you're one of those people that feel like you have no control over Word of Mouth advertising? Oh, I get it, you think that new business just happens all by itself. And, you know what? – it may – but it MAY NOT!

What do your customers want? Which activity is bringing in the business? Do you wonder what to do next to get more customers?

When you "Measure for Success" (survey your customers), you will be better equipped to pick the right strategies that will help your business grow – targeting those advertising dollars on a message that offers the consumer something they're looking for!

Knowing what your customers want and how they feel about your service, helps you develop a game plan, a road map, to guide you through even the toughest times.

It just makes good business sense to not waste your money on the development of new features that your customers don't really care about!

Conserve precious resources. Direct your time and energy on activities that are valued by your customers. . .

Jump start that "Word of Mouth" engine.
Start a campaign tomorrow, and for FREE!

Step 2 – Measure for Success

OK, I understand, that word "campaign" does sound a bit formal – but you don't have to be a Ph.D. in Organizational Effectiveness to do a survey tomorrow.

Why tomorrow? I need to give you a little time to read the "11% Solution" today, and start your campaign tomorrow!

Congratulations on taking the first step - read "Measure for Success", and then give your customers what they want.

They'll love you for it- and tell all their friends that you care about what they think! (hence the "Word of Mouth" campaign gets started.)

HERE'S HOW! The 3 "NO COST Secrets", The Plan, and Sample Survey Questions below, show you exactly how to "Measure for Success" and start your "Word of Mouth" campaign Today.

The Plan

(3 no cost secrets and

5 sample survey questions)

. . . .

3 no cost secrets

#1 – Collect e-mails

#2 – Register Now for Survey Monkey

#3 – Develop 5 questions

This is how you start an e-mail campaign to better understand the wants and needs of your customers. Why do you want to do this? Because – and I quote Larry Miller, CEO of Sit & Sleep Mattresses with 22 superstores in Southern California:

Step 2 – Measure for Success

"Your Customers Are Your Best Sales People"

If you find out what they want, and then give it to them, they'll reward you by doing your advertising for you.

The "how to" of the 3 NO COST secrets of how to get started on "Measure for Success" is detailed as follows::

#1 – Collect e-mails

You need a list of prospects. So, begin by gathering "fresh" e-mail addresses. An old database doesn't work – you've heard of SPAMMING? The goal here is to show caring & consideration, so don't run the risk of making your past customers angry and annoyed by assuming that you can send them a survey or e-mail.

Here are a couple of easy ideas that you or your staff can do to collect "permission-based" e-mails.

- add an "e-mail" field, or make an e-mail stamp – for your intake/order form for each new customers, and/or
- when someone picks up an order – ask if they "would be willing" to give you their e-mail, and/ or
- conduct outreach phone calls – call your most recent customers (from the last 6 months) to "update your database", confirm their info, and get their permission to add their e-mail address so you can

The 11% Solution

"send them Exclusive coupon offers", etc. for your e-mail customers only.

Collect at least 25 e-mails (statisticians around the world are rolling their eyeballs) – however, the more the better – and type your e-mail addresses into an Excel spreadsheet. Enter each piece of data into a separate column (e.g. "e-mail address", "first name", "last name", etc). Remember: "Permission-based" is the key to collecting e-mails.

#2 – Register Now

Sign up for Survey Monkey or Constant Contact – I've used both, and highly recommend either – for simplicity of use and overall effectiveness.

> **Survey Monkey is free FOREVER up to 100 responses.**
>
>
>
> www.surveymonkey.com/Default.aspx

Step 2 – Measure for Success

Constant Contact is prettier than Survey Monkey, and makes a better impression, but it has a slight learning curve, and it comes with a very low price tag.

Constant Contact also emphasizes that your e-mails are all "permission-based" – which is a good thing.

With my help and the Constant Contact 800#, you'll be sending out spectacular e-mails in no time. (sign up for your FREE 60 day trial at www.theserviceadvisors.com).

Here's another bonus when you use Constant Contact: they have a tool that personalizes the e-mails with the customer's first name. For example, you can send me an e-mail that has the greeting:

"Dear Verena,"

The more personal you can make an e-mail, the more it sounds like you're speaking directly to the customer. That's why it's important to set up your database as I've mentioned above. (see #1 – bullet three)

The 11% Solution

Just copy and paste the URL below into your browser and get started with your

FREE 60 day trial.

www.constantcontact.com/index.jsp?pn=theservicea
dvisors

#3 – Develop 5 questions

Try to keep it to down to 5 questions – more is OK, but absolutely no more than 10. Your questions should be "actionable" - in other words, the questions are constructed so you can "take action" on the responses - and one of the questions should be a "baseline" question. (It stays the same from survey to survey so you can measure your progress.)

Here's a sample of 5 questions you can ask:

1. How did you hear about us?
2. How would you rate our _____?
3. What can we do to improve your shopping experience?
4. How can we make our product/service better?
5. How would you rate your overall satisfaction with ABC company?

Step 2 – Measure for Success

Here are the questions, again, with more detail and the reasons why you should ask them:

1. How did you hear about us?

(Question type: "Multi-Select Multiple Choice")

☐ Newspaper
☐ e-mail
☐ website
☐ Word of Mouth
☐ Other

This question is important because it tells you which of your advertising efforts is valuable. If nobody select "newspaper", then you can stop spending your money on that particular newspaper ad.

2. On a scale of 1 to 10 (10 being best), how would you rate our (product name or service)?

(Question type: "Rate One Item On A Scale")

1 2 3 4 5 6 7 8 9 10
Not good   **Super good**

You want to ask "rate"-type questions so you can tease out the nuances For example, your goal could be to receive all 8's, 9's & 10's. Why? Because these are the customers who will talk about you and do the advertising for you!

3. What can we do to improve your shopping experience?

(Question type: "Open-ended Text")

–   (Comment box)

[   ]

Asking about the "experience" shows that you care about the customer at every step of the process – from the website, to the phone system, to the parking lot, to the signage, etc.

The tendency will be to "ignore" what a customer says – especially if the comment's suggesting an improvement. One negative comment doesn't mean you should jump to make a change. Just be mindful and know that if one person feels this way, there are 20 others out there who feel the same way, (but just walk away and never say anything)!

4. How can we make our (name the product or service) better?

(Question type: "Open-ended Text")

–   (Comment box)

[   ]

Ever heard of "pride of ownership? It's a powerful thing. Ask any Realtor®.

Step 2 – Measure for Success

I know that you're proud of your product or service. But, there may be an opportunity for improvement that you haven't thought of.

Maybe you're already the best at what you do, but wouldn't you like to hear how you could be even better? So try your darndest to really listen and be open-minded. Try to see the issue from the customer's perspective.

And, finally the last question in your simple survey:

5. **On a scale of 1 to 10 (10 being best), how would you rate your overall satisfaction with ABC company?**

(Question type: "Rate One Item On A Scale".)

1 2 3 4 5 6 7 8 9 10
Not good   **Super good**

Ask this question on every survey, and be careful not to change the wording. Then, it serves as a "baseline" question, and you can closely watch the results to see if the changes you've implemented are actually having a positive effect over time.

So why go to all this effort? (Oh dear, I can hear you start to whine.)

The 11% Solution

First of all, I've given you everything you need to get you started, and thereby, reduced a lot of the time it takes to put a survey together. These questions are generic enough that they can be used to survey customers from any type of business.

Secondly, when you tailor your product or service to what your customer's want - they notice. And what do they do when they notice? That's right. They talk about you.

Here in the Los Angeles area, there is a very successful mattress store called Sit & Sleep. Larry Miller, the owner, built his business with the motto,

"Your Customers Are Your Best Salespeople."

So, can you afford to wait for "Word of Mouth" to happen? You can choose to go the "organic" route – which takes longer – but you might be waiting for a long time, and losing money in the process.

Or you can take action – move the process forward – none of has time to be organic, while our competition is passing us by.

Ask your customers what they want, and then give it to them. Everything else just sort of falls into place naturally if you make this step one of your priorities.

STEP 3

Make it Right

"Take a customer from hell to heaven

In 60 seconds or less"

John Tschohl, International

Customer Service Strategist

When something goes wrong – and it will - how does your business make it go right?

Does saying "I'm sorry" bug you? Do you and/or your staff tend to roll your eyes, feel a little defensive, or make a "snarky" remark, when a customer is unhappy?

I'm sorry for laughing too hard
I'm sorry for not caring
I'm sorry I left you on hold
I'm sorry being demanding
and
I'm sorry for not saying "I'm sorry"
I sorry for saying "I'm sorry"
I'm sorry for not pleasing everyone
I'm sorry for smiling
I'm sorry for not smiling
I'm sorry for walking slow
I'm sorry I'm not blonde

The 11% Solution

Perhaps you already have a "Service Recovery" policy in your procedure manual – and it clearly outlines what steps every employee should follow when there has been a mistake or a customer is, in general, unhappy with the service received or the product purchased.

But, do me a favor - read it again. Does your policy address the human behavior procedure? Would your employee know exactly what to say and how to act should something go wrong?

How do you want your staff to behave when a customer complains?

There is a strategy for turning those complaining customers into fans of your great service. But this takes extra time and attention – why should you bother? Because. . . and I say it again and again. . .

"Your Customers Are Your Best Salespeople"

I just spent some time with my mother-in-law who raved about the personal attention she got from her car dealership. Yes, you heard me right. A car dealership! In fact, she switched dealerships because of the service!

Here's what "grabbed" her.

Her side mirror was broken, so she drove to the dealership to get it fixed – fully expecting to wait and pay for the service.

Step 3 – Make it Right

To her surprise, the salesperson saw her drive onto the lot, and told all the other salespeople, "I've got it guys - This is my customer."

Then the salesperson proceeded to have my mother-in-law's mirror repaired immediately, and at no charge.

Now, you may think this is "smarmy" or not your style, but my mother-in-law – guaranteed – is not only telling me about the great service at this dealership, but she's telling everyone in her bridge group, her clubs, her neighbors - about how glad she is to have made the switch to this new dealership.

Oh, another thing – she specifically tells everyone what the old dealership did wrong!

So, put a smile on the face of that unhappy customer. You may be the owner of a business, or a salesperson, or a clerk at the cash register.

Whoever you are, you have the power to create any unhappy customer into a super loyal fan who does the advertising for you. Now you've exponentially grown your advertising budget – and for NO COST!

Many successful organizations know the power of service recovery in creating the loyal fan of great service. For example, in survey after survey, customer loyalty ranks as one of the top five concerns of CEO's. And here's why:

The 11% Solution

> Studies show that organizations could increase their revenues by 85% if they could retain 5% more of their best customers
>
> Studies also show that it costs 6 times more to get a new customer than it does to keep an existing customer.
>
> Loyal customers tell at least 4 other people about their experiences. Merely satisfied customers most likely tell no one.
>
> Satisfied customers will defect at the slightest prompt. Only extremely satisfied customers are genuinely loyal.
>
> A Xerox-sponsored research project on customer service indicated that merely satisfying customers did not keep them loyal.

Convinced? So, why all the fuss over loyalty?

Simply this. . . Customers that are loyal do business with you again and again – plus, they tell a friend about their experience with your organization. And, so on, and so on . . . creating that no cost advertising buzz that we're all looking for.

OK, that makes sense, so, how do we create the loyal fan of great service?

Step 3 – Make it Right

The easiest way to create loyalty is to convert the dissatisfied customer into a happy camper. So, a complaint is an opportunity – a gold mine, if you will – that offers you, and your staff, an opportunity to create a lifelong customer. But before you charge in . . . realize that there's a strategy to this complaint thing.

> **Research shows that customers who complaint receive an apology only about 50% of the time. That's about half as often as they should.**

I'll bet that you're reading this and thinking about a time that you received poor service, or you've been a disappointed in how your complaint was handled.

Did the customer service rep make you feel ridiculous, embarrassed, or even worse – did they argue with you and point out what you "should have done?" Would a sincere apology have made a difference?

I know I've had many such poor service experiences, and I've happily told my stories for many years. Why? Because they could have been resolved, or avoided all together, with just a little care and concern that I was unhappy.

In fact, you can read about my favorite poor service story, and meet Rox"E" the Doxie at:

www.theserviceadvisors.com/The-Problem.html.

The 11% Solution

There are few things more disappointing than when a mistake is not corrected skillfully-- especially when it would have taken only a moment to correct the problem and "Make it Right."

The skill to "Make It Right" (Service Recovery done right) includes four steps. These steps are simple, and guaranteed to convert an unhappy customer into a super loyal fan who tells everyone how wonderful you are.

1. **Apologize sincerely**
2. **Correct the mistake**
3. **Take an extra step**
4. **Follow-up**

OK – so now you know the four steps, but there's a method to my madness, and the 4 steps are most successful when done correctly. (And don't be tempted to save time by skipping one!)

1.   Apologize sincerely

A sincere apology not only acknowledges the mistake, it indicates that it will be fixed - regardless of who made the error.

(IMPORTANT: If you don't apologize, the customer will shut down and just continue to argue with you - never letting you solve their problem – no matter how hard you try!)

What is "sincere?" "Sincere" uses an Empathy statement, and it sounds like:

> **(Apologize):** "I'm so sorry this didn't meet your expectations.
>
> **(Empathy statement):** From your description, it sounds to me like we've given you confusing information.

Or

> **(Apologize):** "I'm very sorry –
>
> **(Empathy statement):** I can see how this situation has been frustrating for you.

2. Correct the mistake –

If a solution is not obvious, ask the customer how he/she would like to have the problem solved. Give options and let the customer choose the solution. This restores power to the customer and is an important step in helping them "let go" of their anger and frustration.

The 11% Solution

Remember, you're not giving away your power. You're still very much in control of the situation.

So add steps 1 & 2 together and you get:

> 1. **Apologize:** "I'm very sorry – I can see how this situation has been frustrating for you.
> 2. **Correct the mistake** – "May I make a suggestion for how to set this right."

3. Take an extra step –

For example, is a customer complaining about the long wait? Buy some vouchers from the donut shop next door, and send the customer over to have a cup of coffee & a muffin while you're working on resolving the problem.

Restaurants can provide free drinks or appetizers. Hotels can upgrade to suites at no extra charge. Car dealerships can provide no-cost loaner vehicles. Airlines can offer passengers first-class upgrades. Internet service providers can waive fees. The list goes on and on

Whatever type of organization you belong to, I guarantee, there is something you can offer to a customer as a token of appreciation, and to emphasize that you are appreciative of their future business.

Note to self: Ask your staff: What can my company offer as a token of appreciation?

Step 3 – Make it Right

So steps 1, 2 and 3 sound like this:

> 1. **Apologize:** "I'm very sorry, Ms. Somer – I can see how this situation has been frustrating for you.
> 2. **Correct the mistake** – "May I make a suggestion for how to set this right."There are a couple of options. You pick the one that's right for you."
> 3. **Take an extra step** – "While we're waiting for "x,y,z" to get finished, please have a seat, let me get you a cup of coffee (or bottle of water) and a magazine. We'll put a rush on "x,y,z", and let me know if I can help you with anything.

Now we're ready to add the icing to the cake. The next, and final step to service recovery done right is "Follow-up", and it goes like this:

4. Follow-up –

Provide the customer with your business card, and a number where they can reach you.

The 11% Solution

This is important to the process, so go ahead. Do something wild – like give out your personal cell phone number!

I have personal experience with this step. I was presenting to a group of 200 physicians, who were skeptical about the personalized service and attention I was promising to them.

I gave them added assurance that any problem they had, I would handle personally – and I gave out my personal cell phone number. I actually pulled out the phone, and read the number to them. Then challenged them to call me right then and there, to make sure they had the correct number.

Those rascals. They actually couldn't believe I was giving out my personal cell phone number, so several of them dialed me, and to their surprise, the number was correct!

Making sure the customer can contact you if the problem isn't corrected to their satisfaction is critical to gaining trust and creating loyalty.

So, let's add up all the steps with examples of what to say:

Step 3 – Make it Right

1. **Apologize:** "I'm very sorry, Ms. Somer. I can see how this situation has been frustrating for you.
2. **Correct the mistake** – "May I make a suggestion for how to set this right? We have a couple of options. You pick the one that's right for you."
3. **Take an extra step** – "While we're waiting for "x,y,z" to get finished, please have a seat, let me get you a cup of coffee (or bottle of water) and a magazine. We'll put a rush on "x,y,z", and there will be no charge today for the service."
4. **Follow-up:** "Ms. Somer, here's my business card with my name and number on it. And, I've also included my personal cell phone number, just in case you have further problems with "x,y,z, you can call me anytime."

I understand the cell phone thing can be very scary, but people actually have great respect for your time, and won't use it unless there's an absolute emergency. I had one physician – out of 200 – call me once.

Let me just back track a minute and talk to you about "the apology" piece of the 4 steps to Service Recovery done right.

The 11% Solution

It can be very tough for some folks (perhaps even you!) to say "I'm sorry." These two little words don't mean that you're admitting any kind of liability, or that you've contributed to the problem, or that you've failed in some way.

In no way does saying, "I'm sorry" mean that you are somehow to blame. It simply means that you're acknowledging that things aren't going well for the customer, and you're truly "sorry" that they feel distressed &/or inconvenienced by the situation.

I'm the first one to acknowledge that many of us were brought up to believe that an apology is an admission of guilt. However, recent studies have suggested that clients appreciate candor from their professional advisors and recognize that even the most hardworking and capable professionals make honest mistakes.

For example, as Peter Bregman wrote in his article in the Harvard Business Review, "I want you to apologize", "When the University of Michigan Health System experimented with full disclosure, existing claims and lawsuits dropped from 262 in 2001 to 83 in 2007." Now those are numbers to pay attention to.

Another tip: No matter who you think is at fault – it could be you, the customer or another department – NEVER EVER point it out. Nobody cares who caused the problem, just apologize and fix it. Your colleagues, coworkers - and the customer - will appreciate you for it!

(However, if a co-worker did contribute to the problem, speak to them later, if necessary, and in private.)

Step 3 – Make it Right

"Make It Right!" – But, keep it simple and hassle free!

Give everyone in your organization the power to do what it takes – and, yes, that means empowerment! Anyone, at any time, can be faced with an unhappy customer. And, the "boss" might not be there to coach them through the situation.

Give everyone the power to practice solving the problem on-the-spot, and keep the process hassle free for the customer.

Here's another example of the power of Service Recovery:

One of my clients was really having difficulty with their customer satisfaction scores. They had recently gone through about three different leaders in a 12 month period, and everyone was confused and demoralized – nobody was happy – and could care less about making their customers happy.

As a result, the service was poor, generated lots of complaints, and ate up tons of valuable time of both the staff and the managers. So, I met with the entire team to identify how they could improve.

After hearing them discuss their problems, I recommended that they implement a Service Recovery process. And, in just a few months, they had a huge success.

The leadership was so impressed with their turnaround, that their success was graphed and featured in

The 11% Solution

company posters to recognize their success. Everyone could now see a model of how you could use "service" strategies to turn around customer satisfaction and grow your business.

Note the dotted, vertical line in the graph. This is when we began to meet and implement Service Recovery. The results were immediate and overwhelmingly positive.

> *In less than 1 quarter, this client's scores jumped by almost 7 points. They continued with the process and ended on a high note. In less than 3 quarters, their scores improved by 14.55 points to end at a highly satisfied score of 87.76%.*

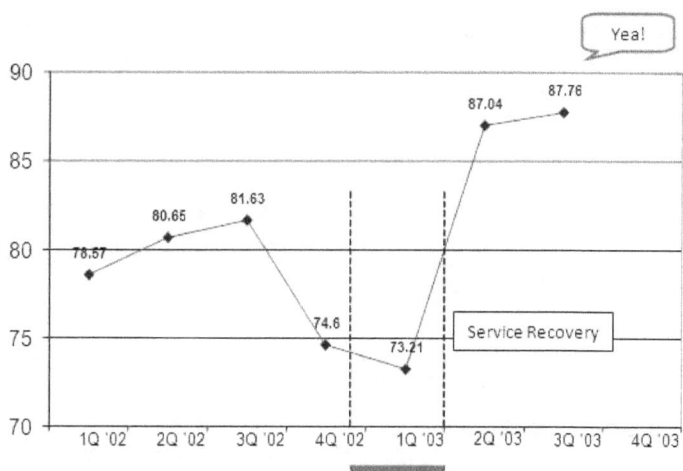

How Service Recovery Improves Customer Satisfaction

In less than 1 quarter, this client's scores jumped by almost 7 points. They continued with the process and ended on a high note. In less than 3 quarters, their scores improved by 14.55 points to end at a highly satisfied score of 87.76%.

Figure 2.0 – Service Recovery Results

Step 3 – Make it Right

When I talk to employees about service recovery, it never fails – one issue always comes up. What do you do about the customer who is verbally abusive, or throws things at you, or in general attacks you personally.

Here's what I know from my 25 years of experience in dealing with sometimes really angry customers.

When a customer is unhappy, they attack. And, it's very easy for anyone who feels attacked to get "hooked."

Getting 'hooked" is just what it sounds like. You've taken the bait and gotten a sharp wire in your cheek, because you've reacted to the verbal abuse or denigrating remarks that can sometimes spew out of an angry customer's mouth!

I use these words to coach my staff into staying calm: "Remember, the degree of "upset" is in direct proportion to the customer's level of contribution to the problem." In other words: the more one has contributed towards creating the problem, the madder one gets.

Let me explain further. Let's say that a customer, Mrs. Jones, has forgotten to pay her bill on time, and now she's really, really angry that Company ABC (you) shut off her power. She's called to cuss and swear and, in general, make whoever is on the other end as miserable as she can.

The customer, Mrs. Jones, has made a major contribution to the problem by not paying her bill on time. So, her anger is off the charts, and directed at the first unlucky person to be the target of her wrath.

She's absolutely furious that she's in this situation, and she won't recognize or acknowledge that she had a big part to play in this unpleasant scenario. The idea isn't even a part of her consciousness. She's just so mad she can't see straight!

But, when you get defensive and ruffled at the customer's bad behavior, the customer wins, becomes victorious and all-powerful because they've "hooked" you, gotten you to act unprofessionally, and buy into their bad behavior.

Mrs. Jones will rejoice in telling a story that makes you look like "the wicked Company ABC", and portrays her as a victim of Company ABC's (your) staff and (your) policies.

But, we're not done, yet. You can do all the service recovery steps perfectly, but then you make one fatal error. You point out how the customer contributed to the situation. \

It goes something like this:

"Mrs. Jones, I'm so sorry that this situation has gotten out of hand. It must be very frustrating for you to try and maintain a household with no power. If you have cash, check, a debit card or even a credit to make payment now, I can get the situation corrected immediately. And, here's my business card to give you a point of contact if the problem is not resolved to your satisfaction.

And, here's the kicker:

"But, let me point out that you did not make payment this month, and our policy is . . . "

Oh my goodness, and it was all going so well. Just try to point out the problem to Mrs. Jones, and the situation will quickly spin out of control. She is very likely to storm off just looking for the first person who will listen to her tale of woe, and the employee, will storm into your office either in tears, or so angry they could spit nails!

Mrs. Jones could very likely end up in your office, too!

Now you've spent half your day resolving a customer complaint. All because the employee wanted to be in control, couldn't resist having the last word, and felt it necessary to teach Mrs. Jones a lesson for behaving so badly.

(I mentioned this earlier, but in case you missed it: I used to do a monthly report for an organization on types of complaints received. The most common was a complaint that the staff said, "Our policy is. . . ")

The 11% Solution

Now, you can poke holes in this scenario all you want to, but the issue applies to any company type. Just stay calm and remember to not look for fault – believe me it's everywhere, the customer, the employee, the company policy, etc. And, if you point it out, you've just joined the power struggle.

Just in case you need another example. . .

. . . a customer could be very angry that you didn't deliver an order on time. You find yourself chomping at the bit, because you really want to tell them that they caused the delay by repeatedly changing the order!

Jeesh! Don't they know that they caused the problem! You know it, and I know it, and chances are, the customer knows it, too. But never let the customer know that you know. They'll feel "scolded" and powerless, and this is a sure fire way to add gasoline to the fire.

This situation presents you with the perfect opportunity to role-model great customer service. Just apologize, offer options, and let the customer pick the solution.

You'll be amazed at how well this no-cost solution works to bring customers back from the brink of defection and have a positive impact on your bottom line.

There now, that wasn't so bad, was it? And the bonus is you've just made a super loyal customer that will talk about how you saved the day. And the bonus is - you also role-modeled great service for your staff! Now they're more likely to handle similar situations just like you!

That was simple, right?

Yep – but it does take a little practice. This whole complaint thing can be a little scary – especially for your staff. There can be a lot of fear and anxiety associated with "using your own judgement."

You, for example, are a "decision-maker" on a daily basis, so that makes you very comfortable at routinely solving problems. But, in this case, it's very important that you not jump in with an immediate "fix".

Stand back, and let someone else on your staff give it a try. You'll be close by in the background for encouragement and support.

Better yet, the staff person who was originally involved with the customer should be responsible for solving their complaint. This isn't intended to "punish" the staff person for anything, but it has a calming effect on the customer. Especially when they understand that you don't want to irritate them further by making them tell their story all over again to someone new!

Your staff can learn how to handle these issues, and they'll love the opportunity to learn a leadership skill. You'll also reap the rewards of delegating the process to them, because you will have gained their trust, freed up your time and limited constant interruptions throughout the day.

The 11% Solution

Giving staff the freedom to make their own decisions is a great leadership technique, and will do amazing things to make your day go more smoothly.

So, talk through the process, establish a few guidelines (for example, when they're first trying out the process, give them the authority to "fix" a problem however they choose.

If it will make you more comfortable, tell them that they only need your permission if they're going to spend over $25 for the "fix") – and then follow through.

Ask staff how it's going every week for at least 8 weeks. (You have to repeat an action at least 7 times for it to become habit).

And, whether the outcome is good or could use some improvement, remember to always recognize and thank the individual for applying the service recovery principles.

Complaints are gold mines, so greet them "head on." They create so many opportunities for you and the team to connect and learn new skills. Plus you've just converted an unhappy customer into a fan of your great service!

(I just heard a Buck Go BANG!)

Step 3 – Make it Right

This process is easy, but when first introduced, it can also be overwhelming. So, if you forget everything else, at a minimum remember to apologize. I promise you, everything will fall into place naturally. It's a good day!

STEP 4

Look Your Best

"The way to gain a good reputation

is to endeavor to be what you desire to appear".

Socrates

Would you hire you?

Take a look around

Is your space cluttered?

Can your customers see your messy desk? If so, they might be thinking:

The 11% Solution

"Is my order going to drop through the cracks?"

I'm just saying – a glimpse of a messy work area makes it very easy for a customer to jump to the wrong conclusion – they draw conclusions about who you are – it translates to the product or service you're associated with - and the downhill slide begins. Everything possible goes wrong, and you lose the customer forever.

Now, I fully expect you "messy-deskers" to give me some push back on this issue. For example, you could argue that you're a very busy person, and your office reflects that you're processing lots of orders!

Well, that may be a reasonable argument, but remember

SERVICE and QUALITY

are inextricably linked.

And SERVICE includes everything that gives off an "impression". . .

EVERYTHING!

This "impression" is what laymen use to judge quality. Now, you messy desk guys may be feeling picked on, and you're already arming yourself with excuses about how unfair it is to judge a person's product or service based on the look of their office space.

Step 4 – Look Your Best

But it turns out that the conclusions we draw about who people are, from the office they keep, are actually pretty accurate perceptions. So if your messy desk is making your customers feel uncertain about doing business with you – you really can't blame them, can you?

Researchers have proven that a person's first impression is pretty accurate.

For example, Penelope Trunk is CEO and author of Brazen Careerist, a career management tool for next-generation professionals. She writes about "messy desk syndrome" in an August 2010 BNet article entitled "Managing Your Career By Managing The Stuff on Your Desk."

Ms. Trunk quotes the guy that studies this stuff obsessively - Sam Gosling, a professor of social psychology at the University of Texas and the author of "Snoop: What Your Stuff Says About You."

Professor Gosling's research cites a study from 1942. As the United States was entering World War II, the US Government was trying to figure out the best way to identify people who would make good spies.

One of the aptitude exams the government developed was the "Belongings Test", in which candidates had to draw conclusions about a man based purely on items in his bedroom: clothes, a timetable, a ticket receipt, etc.

Professor Gosling concludes that the government test was successful. He states: "The test works because people are good at drawing conclusions based on people's stuff."

If possible, and if your work area is visible to the customer, make the piles of papers into neat stacks. This will, at least, give me the impression that you're organized, and lead me to believe that you won't lose my order!

A Moment of Truth – and More On Drawing Conclusions

Here's an example of how Service & Quality are inextricably linked.

I was on a reputable airline that had a scheduled stop to refuel in a country south of the border. While we were waiting for the refueling to commence, we heard a clanging noise coming from outside on the tarmac.

We looked out the window and saw a mechanic (?) whacking away on the landing gear with a wrench!

No one explained what was going on, and we were left to draw our own conclusions.

Uh oh!

Step 4 – Look Your Best

Do you really want your customers to view your messy desk, flip flops, poor signage, etc., and draw their own conclusions?

Let's say I give you a break on the messy desk thing, and ignore it for the time being . . . But, how about asking yourself:

"How many other Moments of Truth are between you and "The Sale"

Some "moments" that deserve your attention: The directions on your voice mail, the signs taped to your windows, parking, signage, and the name badges hung down by the belly button in a font that's unreadable. These are all critical "moments" in the service chain.

You sold them once, can you sell them again?

YES, you can!

Take stock of the perceptions you may be conveying. Be critical of yourself and others. Don't let your customers draw the wrong conclusions and walk out the door never to come back again.

The 11% Solution

3 Things That Will Cause Your Customers to Leave Forever. . .

1. Confuse Them

Have the directions/signage been "tested?"

You may be frustrating your customers before they even meet you! Show them you care enough to pay attention to the details. "Test" your messages with someone who is using your service for the first time. Ask them if the messages and directions make sense.

Are the messages friendly and welcoming?

Is there a reason for the door to be locked during the lunch hour? Hello? I can hear you inside the office, and I'm patiently waiting out here in the hall!

Can you read the "Open" / "Closed" sign on your front door clearly from the parking lot?

Please don't make me get out of the car and hike to your front door only to find that you're closed every other Friday!

Step 4 – Look Your Best

Is it easy to identify the staff?

Is the first name on your ID badge in really big font? Does it hang low from your neck on a lanyard? (I personally don't like squinting at someone's bellybutton trying to make out their name.) Even a casual uniform of t-shirts and tennis shoes needs a readable name tag.

2. Treat them like they're at the County Fair

Are the bathrooms well maintained?

Yuck! There's nothing quite like empty soap dispensers, no paper towels and sticky floors to send a message about how much you care about quality!

3. Take them for granted

Is your area noisy?

TV's are great, but think about it - not everyone likes Jerry Springer.

These are a few Moments of Truth that are common to all businesses, and represent decision-making moments for the customer. They'll gladly overlook the "messy desk" syndrome if you show caring and concern regarding the items above.

Keep in mind - It costs 6 times more to capture a new customer as it does to keep an old one!

Pay close attention to these little "moments", and I guarantee, they're gonna say:

"You're Hired!"

STEP 5

Share the Love

"People will forget what you said, people will forget what you did, but people will never forget how you made them feel."

Maya Angelou, Author and Poet

Aaah. . . Share the Love, aka, Recognition. I get all warm and fuzzy just thinking about it. But, it can also turn out to be the biggest nightmare you've ever encountered!

Recognition can backfire, it can go unappreciated, and it can go

Thank You
I really
appreciated
it when
you . . .

The 11% Solution

so badly that you never want to do it again!

Wait – weren't we just talking "warm and fuzzy?" How can this happen over something as positive and well-intended as praising people for a job well done?"

I've had to implement more than one recognition program in my time, and I finally got tired of doing all this work just to have it fall flat. I had to ask myself why I wasn't getting the long term, sustainable, results that I (and my bosses) had expected.

Maybe I had been taking this recognition thing for granted. Saying "Thank You" was a very powerful phrase in its own right, but I suspected there was more. So, before I implemented a recognition program again, I finally got smart and realized that I needed to do some research.

I was at a conference in Boston, perusing the library offerings at the hotel, and I ran across some information in a book entitled "If Disney Ran Your Hospital," by Fred Lee.

I'll never forget Chapter 9. It shared a simple little story that made such a huge difference in the way I approached recognition that I want to share it with you.

Now, please understand that it's been about 6 or 7 years since I've read the actual book, so I might have some of the details backwards.

Basically, it recounted the story of a man who was the target of bad behavior. Every day, a group of young boys hurled epithets at him as they passed his house on their way to and from school.

Really tired of being the subject of all this daily abuse, the man offered the boys a quarter, every day, just to leave him alone.

Voila! It worked like magic! No more name-calling – no more anything! When the boys passed his house, they were all as quiet as church mice.

Things went on very smoothly, and as time passed, the man stopped giving the daily quarter. Well, you can probably guess what happened...

The boys started up with the bad behavior, again.

Do rewards really create loyalty?

So, what are we supposed to do? A lot of our recognition includes giving a reward like a plaque, a trophy, or a gift certificate for exceptional performance. Yet, these items are small potatoes when compared to some rewards. Consider this...

What would some companies do if their budgets could no longer handle the luxury vacations or annual bonuses. If they stopped giving "rewards" for good performance, it's highly likely that the desired behaviors would stop.

The 11% Solution

Look at the recent debacle with AIG. They were at the heart of a global meltdown, received millions in government bailouts, but did they still give out bonuses?

You bet they did. Even after experiencing the wrath of the public and the scathing press. Their response to the criticism was, and I'm paraphrasing, "We won't be able to compete, all our good people will jump ship."

Aha! What I'm hearing is that there's no loyalty to AIG! And why should there be? When you can go around the corner to the next large firm and receive even more luxurious vacations and bigger bonuses!

This is what happens when an entire industry is based on a system of rewards – and huge ones, at that.

So, what's the answer?
Should we give rewards or not?

You may have noticed that this step does NOT include the word "rewards" anywhere in the title. And, there's a very good reason for this.

Most programs are called "Rewards & Recognition." Think about it. The word "Rewards" always comes first.

I once tried re-naming a program to "Recognition, "Re-enforcement, & Rewards." (Putting the word "Rewards" last.) Ha! That went over like a lead balloon! And even though I felt very passionate about the symbolism of putting "rewards" last, everyone looked at me like I had lost my marbles!

Whatever the name of your program, I suggest abandoning the word "Rewards" and just renaming it to a "Recognition" program. Why?

The main focus of your appreciation should be based on Recognition. Never Rewards. Because, when you take away the reward, the behavior stops.

Hmmm . . maybe. . .but still not convinced? I don't blame you, so here's another opinion to support my argument.

> In a 1995 study of Kepner-Tregoe, a training and development company, **only forty percent** of North American workers surveyed said they received any recognition for a job well-done, and about the same percentage reported that their outstanding individual accomplishments were never acknowledged.
>
> In the same study, **only fifty percent** of the managers said that they gave recognition for high performance.
>
> Yet, when asked, **ninety-six percent** of the workers in the study agreed with the statement "I get a lot of satisfaction out of knowing I've done a good job."

Do me a favor, read those three paragraphs again.

Can you believe that only 50% of managers give recognition for high performance?

The 11% Solution

I can. I've worked for too many clients (and had too many bosses!) that don't emphasize recognition or hold the managers accountable for giving out recognition. Everyone feels just fine with their recognition system that's impersonal and relies on rewards. It's easier that way.

How so??

Because, recognition takes time. You have to put thought into it, be specific about how the behavior helped the customer or colleague, keep records of personal preferences, hand-write a personal thank you note, etc. All this takes time.

Now, to be fair, it's not all bad. I have been associated with recognition programs that were very effective, mainly because they focused on appreciation, and held their managers accountable via an annual employee survey. But, guess what, I designed those programs. So, I'm just a little bit biased!

I told you earlier that I did a lot of research on how to build an effective recognition program. After reading pages and pages, study after study, I distilled tons of information into the following six principles that will make any recognition program effective, robust and heartfelt.

Measureable – Timely – Personal

Focused on Appreciation – Non-Competetive

Linked to Values

Step 5 – Share the Love

So, I'll ask again: "Should we give rewards or not?"

There is an answer, and it can be done. But, if you currently use a system of "rewards" for recognizing your staff, and you want to stop, it MAY be perceived as a "take away." So be ready to take some "push back", commit some time, and proceed with caution.

It is very reasonable and totally justified, to tell staff that you have to trim costs by streamlining your "rewards." Review the budget with them so everyone understands the ramifications and the cost savings, and start to substitute no cost/low cost "tokens of appreciation." This allows you to start to minimize the rewards, gradually.

Substitute any minimized reward with tons of recognition.

And, don't forget to set the right expectations for any new staff that you bring on board. Let them know about your system for recognizing good performance up front, during the orientation process. Set clear goals, and link recognition to performance (values).

In summary, my recommendation is to build your "recognition" program using "Tokens of Appreciation." "Tokens" are acceptable, because they imply a nominal $$ amount, if anything. And, if you don't have the budget to continue giving a $10 gift card, taking away this "token" won't be as noticeable, as a $100 gift certificate.

The 11% Solution

Here's a good rule of thumb: "Spend a dollar on the prize, but a thousand on the praise."

The most powerful part of any recognition you give is not the "token", it's the "meaning" behind it. If you feel more comfortable giving a reward, keep the rewards to a "token of appreciation."

I'm sure you've heard it said before, "recognition is powerful." You do not have to spend a lot of money, but it does take time. And, it has to be personal and meaningful. If you do it right, people will remember the feeling you gave them for years to come.

So, I prefer to stay away from tokens all together. They can cause divisiveness amongst the staff and feelings of preferential treatment. I prefer no cost ways of recognition that are customized to the individual. For example:

- Congratulations in front of the staff
- Tell the Story – (stories are better remembered than statistics)
- Paper certificates (templates are on the internet)
- Postings on bulletin boards
- Pictures
- Newsletters
- Handwritten Thank You cards (my personal fave)
- Cook for the staff
- Send a note of thanks to the family
- Customize the recognition to the individual - Remember preferences (Allergic to strawberries? Doesn't like cheesecake?)

Step 5 – Share the Love

Remember, some people, and certain cultures, don't like public recognition at all. They find it embarrassing.

And, just passing out cookies and water doesn't do diddly – however, if you tell people why you're passing out cookies and water – you'll get some bang for your buck! (There's that catchy phrase again!)

STEP 6

Hire for the Heart

"You can have the best service philosophy in the world, but if you don't have great players to execute it, you've lost the game."

Jack Mitchell, author, "Hug Your Customers"

Getting the right person "on the bus", and "in the right seat" is the key to service success.

So, no matter what you're selling – beanbags, coffee cups or commercial real estate, if you are ever in the position to hire someone, this step applies to you.

The 11% Solution

I'm sure you've heard this before. . .

"Hire for Attitude; Train for Skill"

But, how do you get the right people "on the bus?" That, my friend, is the $64,000 question!

In an August, 1996 article written by Peter Carbonara for the magazine "Fast Company", Mr. Carbonara states the cold, hard facts:

> "The all-too-common reality, in far too many companies, is that hiring processes are poorly designed and shabbily executed."

Mr. Carbonara further illustrates his point using a quote from Alan Davidson, an industrial psychologist in San Diego whose clients include Chevron, Merrill Lynch, and the Internal Revenue Service.

Step 6 – Hire for the Heart

So, if you don't believe me or Mr. Carbonara, perhaps Mr. Davidson has the pedigree that will convince you when he says:

> "The overarching idea is that you hire hard and then manage easy. . . that means doing a lot of work up front."

OK. That sounds right on, and I agree wholeheartedly with this statement. Plus, he's certainly got the credentials to back up his opinion. But, why is hiring for attitude so important? . . .

Because, you can always train a person how to do a job, but you can't change their heart, their soul, their outlook on life and the way they form relationships with others.

I use a 5-step process to hire for the heart. But, I was listening to The Dave Ramsey show recently, and heard Dave talking about the interviewing process. Dave is a self-made millionaire who has his own radio talk show, Cable TV show, and has built his own little empire of 300 employees. He uses 12 steps, and said he interviews a person 10, 15, maybe 20 times prior to making a decision.

Even if you interview an applicant 50 times, is this a guarantee that you'll always hire the "right" person?

Unfortunately, the answer is "no." However, there are things you can do that will increase your

The 11% Solution

chances of finding the employee that turns out to be an absolute gem.

But, before I tell you how to tackle this issue, let me share with you a recent experience I had with helping a small business hire a new employee. (The names and job descriptions have been changed to protect the innocent.)

The owners were in the market to hire an entry-level person that would provide much needed back-up and support to their senior staff person. They obligingly followed the process I recommended, which included setting the right service expectations, and including everyone in the hiring process.

We decided, as a group, what to ask during the interview, and invited the applicant into the workroom to begin the process.

I had previously coached this team (comprised of me, the 2 owners and the Senior Coordinator) in developing a series of questions designed to elicit the applicant's work habits. Why is this important?. . .

. . . Because past performance is the best predictor
of future performance.

Everything about the applicant was looking good. He gave examples of how he used customer service strategies to recover unhappy customers, he always put the customer first, and he had the requisite skill level. Even I thought he was pretty near perfect!

Step 6 – Hire for the Heart

Then, at the very end of this 60 minute interview, he surprised everyone by telling us that he liked to leave the workplace – at a moment's notice – to attend to babysitting issues, a soccer match, etc.

Even though some would agree that he clearly had his priorities in the right place, this operation needed him to be there to provide "back-up" to their Senior Coordinator.

It was disappointing, but we all agreed that we didn't even need to go further. We had to "pass" on what seemed to be almost a perfect fit.

What seemed like a lengthy, tedious, overkill of a 60 minute interview process spent on an entry level person, ended up saving the owners countless hours (and dollars) in training an individual who would never meet their needs.

So, I initially concluded that the small business owners had a valuable experience in using the process I recommended. I mean, I just saved them big bucks by avoiding an investment in a person who didn't meet their needs, right?

Not so fast. . . They never used the process again. They simply couldn't tolerate the amount of work it took up front, and their sense of urgency trumped using what appeared (they perceived) to be a waste of time.

They just didn't feel that the time spent to interview (1 hour at most) was worth it for an entry level position.

The 11% Solution

Weeks later, they still needed to hire someone, so they reverted to their past practice. They hired a person who was recommended by a friend at church. This applicant gave them all the right answers – over the phone – sight unseen.

They never called references or included the staff in the process, and as a result, spent hours and dollars on training an individual who struggled with the service AND technical aspects of the job.

Nice guy, but three months later, he just didn't show up for work one day. He didn't call, he didn't write. . . just left them high and dry.

Because they had invested so much time and effort in training, they couldn't afford to go through the whole process again, so they went without.

They continued to miss deadlines – and as customers became disappointed, the store became less and less busy. Each time I visited, the job board had fewer and fewer orders on it. The downward slide had begun.

On the other hand, I consulted with a medical group who had the need to hire, yet again, an entry level person. I had been working with them for months to improve their customer satisfaction scores, and they had been hugely successful in the process.

They now had to hire a new person, and they were very sensitive to getting the right "fit" for their department – someone who shared the same service philosophy as the rest of the staff, and would help them maintain or improve their service scores.

They took the "Hiring for the Heart" philosophy very seriously, and were extremely disciplined in following the process I recommended. They also heavily involved staff in the interview process.

They interviewed an applicant who had all the necessary skills, had outstanding credentials, and had a positive work history with several reputable institutions.

But, something was missing. The applicant didn't seem as serious about "service" as the rest of the team. They all agreed, the applicant was not as customer-focused as they would have liked.

Even though they were understaffed and desperately needed the help, the staff and the manager of the department decided, together, to wait until they could find a person with not only the right skill set, but with the right attitude.

And, yes, this was for an entry-level position. But everyone realized how critical this "frontline" position was to maintaining customer-satisfaction.

Several months passed, but they remained true to their convictions, and found the perfect applicant who had both the right experience, and the "heart" that "fit" with their newly-adopted customer service philosophy.

As a result, they protected their customer satisfaction improvements, strengthened the spirit of the team, and sent a message to everyone that they were VERY serious about "getting the right person on the bus."

Their service scores continued to improve, and they were recognized at a company staff meeting as a "Best Practice" department.

Let's get back to the "5 Easy Steps to Recruiting & Hiring" process. I've used these 5 steps over and over again, and they've never failed me.

Have I hired a "clunker" every now and then? Yep. But, no more than twice in 25 years of hiring – because I use the 5 Easy steps to Recruiting and Hiring.

However, there's just no guarantee – an applicant can be less than truthful, and have all the right answers. But, overall, the process has been well worth the time spent. And, why should you want to go through this process?

Because, all employees are responsible for servicing your customers.

This recruiting & hiring process applies to everyone from the maintenance crew to the security guards. I've worked with clients who have more complaints about their security guards than their phone staff. So, when you bring someone on board, keep in mind – everyone is in sales and can make or break your profit margin.

And let me offer a side note - I spent many years in a corporate environment – aka "union shop." Although both my parents were union employees, (and I

Step 6 – Hire for the Heart

don't know how my family would have made it without the protections of the union), it can be a very challenging environment to work in.

It's the antithesis of being an entrepreneur. But, working within those confines can teach you some valuable lessons that are applicable to small business as well as corporate workplaces.

And, if ever you're in the uncomfortable position of having to "counsel" someone regarding poor performance, or (heaven forbid) you have to fire someone due to performance issues, just remember: we live in a very litigious environment.

It doesn't matter how deep (or shallow) your pockets, you can get sued at the drop of a hat for "wrongful termination." So, for your protection, refer to this process - it can be a life-saver.

Recruiting & Hiring for Service
5 Easy Steps

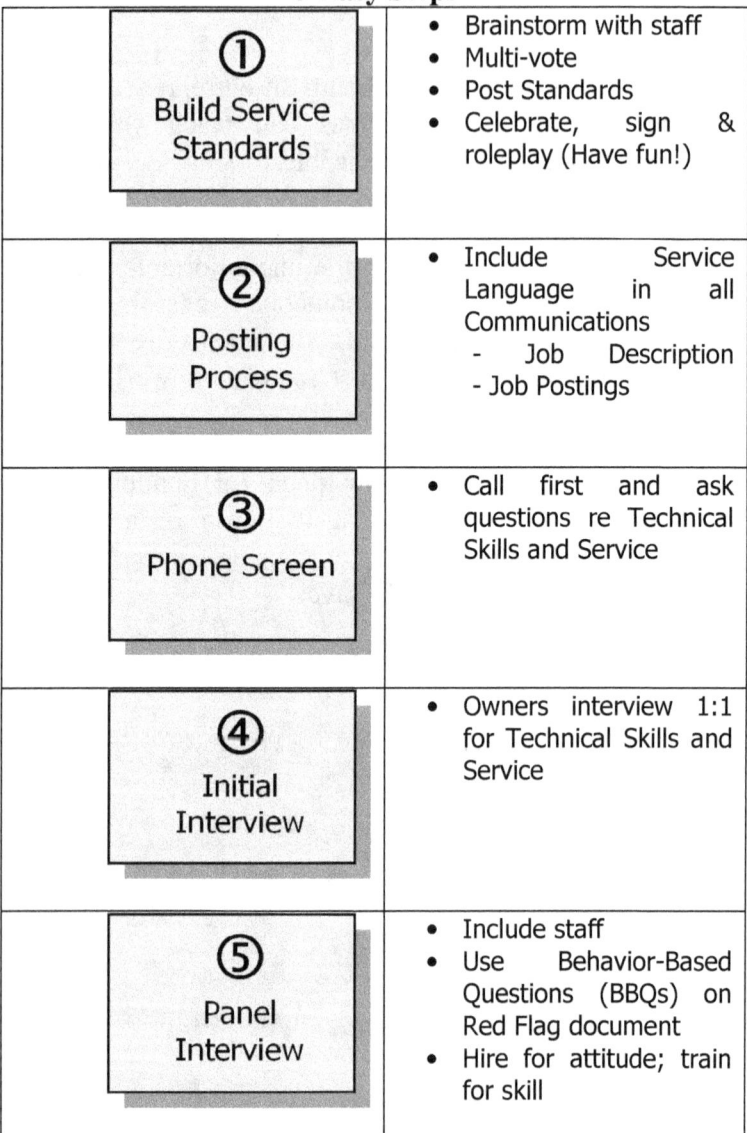

① Build Service Standards	• Brainstorm with staff • Multi-vote • Post Standards • Celebrate, sign & roleplay (Have fun!)

②
Posting
Process
	• Include Service Language in all Communications
	  - Job Description
	  - Job Postings

③ Phone Screen	• Call first and ask questions re Technical Skills and Service
④ Initial Interview	• Owners interview 1:1 for Technical Skills and Service
⑤ Panel Interview	• Include staff • Use Behavior-Based Questions (BBQs) on Red Flag document • Hire for attitude; train for skill

Figure 3.0 – 5 Easy Steps

Step 6 – Hire for the Heart

I'm going to take you through each step listed above and explain the method behind my madness. And, if this seems like a lot of work – keep thinking of the money that you're "leaving on the table" due to unhappy customers. What would it mean to your bottom line to recapture 11% of revenue?

Also, prepping the house to be painted is always the most time consuming and labor-intensive part of the process. But, once you've done it, it's invaluable, priceless, worth every minute –you've saved tons of money and the paint job lasts for years.

Huh? Whah? Why?

Southwest, Ritz Carlton, Nordstrom – sound familiar? These are the big dogs, and legendary for their customer service. Clearly, these companies know the value of great service and the power of "word of mouth" advertising.

They also know that hiring the best people is critical to their success. But, when they're in the market for a new employee, how do they know if they've found a person that's the right "fit" for their company?

The 11% Solution

They've spent years building a brand based on the way they treat their customers, and they're not about to forfeit their reputation based on a few poor customer interactions. They know that it takes just one unhappy customer for the negative "word of mouth" to spread like wildfire.

So, how do they hire the kind of person that's going to demonstrate the care and concern for their customers? Someone who will perpetuate their legend?

Better yet, how does the applicant know what the company expects?

Because, Revco, Disney and UPS all set Service Standards. They know that if you want to hire the best, and be the leader of the pack, you have to set clear expectations about the kind of Service you promise the customer.

This works for the little guys, too. I set service standards for my departments & businesses, and I wouldn't be caught hiring (or training for that matter) without them.

Service Standards tell everyone, customers and staff, right up front, exactly what to expect and how to perform.

Service Standards should leave nothing to question or interpretation.

There's no better way to be crystal clear about what you expect than by building Service Standards.

Step 6 – Hire for the Heart

Then share them with the world - your customers, your staff, and your applicants.

You know I'm always saying: "What does that look like?" And, I'll bet you might be saying the same thing about Service Standards.

So, to help you and your staff move through the process, I've also given you some brief descriptions of brainstorming and multi-voting, as well as a adding some examples of the finished "Service Standards" product.

Take a crack at building your own Service Standards. Follow the bullet points outlined in the 5 Easy Steps and get started today!

Okay, so the first thing to do is pull everyone together and show everyone a sample or two of what you're talking about.

To help you and your staff visualize the process, and get inspired, I've added links to the Service Standards of Disney

www.mouseplanet.com/6978/Disney_Service_Basics

and Ritz-Carlton

www.corporate.ritzcarlton.com/en/About/GoldStandards.htm#service

On the following pages is a sample of Service Standards written by 1 of my clients.

ABC Company Service Standards

*T*AKE *I*NITIATIVE

*T*AKE *R*ESPONSIBILITY

Make a Positive First Impression

Smile and make eye contact.

Be friendly and professional.

Introduce yourself – give name and role.

Anticipate Needs

Be proactive – act first, offer assistance.

Keep customers informed – explain problems and delays.

Offer options.

Ask How You Can Help

Find out what customers want.

Listen attentively.

Be sensitive to special needs.

Assume Ownership

Follow through on commitments.

Know your limits.

Let customers know how they can get back to you if a problem arises.

Solve Problems

Solve the problem or provide options.

Use co-workers to help you solve problems.

Communicate resolution in a timely manner.

Resolve Conflict

Resolve conflict in private.

Focus on the behavior and not the person.

Step 6 – Hire for the Heart

Initiate Service Recovery

Ask customers what else you can help them with.

Do what you can to make your customers happy.

Give Information

Let customers know who, what, when, where, and how.

Ask if a customer or coworker understands or has questions.

If unable to resolve the problem privately, seek assistance from uninvolved co-worker or supervisor.

Demonstrate Competency

Provide service in an accurate, competent manner.

TAKE CARE

TAKE PRIDE

Protect Privacy and Confidentiality

Watch what you say and where you say it.

Show Respect

Ask for and use customer's title and last name.

Don't talk down or use jargon.

Be prompt and timely.

Maintain Your Environment

Keep your work area clean.

Minimize the noise levels.

Be Professional

Dress and conduct yourself professionally.

Conduct personal business on personal time.

The 11% Solution

Understand Differences

Treat purchasers and, co-workers with value.

Acknowledge cultural differences.

Follow language interpretation guidelines.

Show Empathy

Be patient and project a caring attitude.

Accept, don't judge.

Support Your Team

Get to know your teammates, anticipate their needs.

Be open to feedback.

Cooperate with others to deliver excellent service.

Promote Our Business

Speak well of your co-workers and your company.

Share successes and mistakes so others can learn.

WOW your customers.

Always Be Courteous

Figure 4.0 – Service Standards

Step 6 – Hire for the Heart

When you compare the list of Service Standards developed by Disney and Ritz-Carlton to those of my client, you can really see the difference. People don't always get the hang of it the first time around. The important part is to recognize your team for participating in the process.

Just keep encouraging your team to try and be as specific as possible. Remember, a new employee should be able to read your Service Standards and know just how to act to be a successful member of your team - and, how you expect them to treat your customers.

Make copies of these 3 sets of service standards for everyone in the team.

After looking at the 3 sets of service standards offered here, ask your team to highlight the standards that they like best, or that they feel are the most important to your customers.

(By the way, it's OK to use someone else's language. Why re-invent the wheel? If they see a Disney Service Standard that fits your business, by all means - use it!)

Combine your favorite standards, and any of your own ideas, on one big list. This method of assembling ideas is also known as "Brainstorming."

If you've ever been in a brainstorming session gone wrong – it can leave a really bad taste in your mouth. So, I've listed some of my favorite techniques below.

The 11% Solution

Are you ready? Buy some snacks, get a flip chart and a magic marker, and let's get started!

Brainstorm with staff

Include everyone

I like to go around the room, in order, and get at least one idea from each person present. Otherwise, you're likely to get someone who'll dominate (and, thereby, intimidate) others who aren't as vocal. This will make your session productive and fun for everyone.

Don't Tolerate Criticism

One of the most important rules is to require everyone to withhold comments and reactions to each other's ideas. Even an eye roll can stifle creativity: if people are worried that others are judging their ideas, they'll probably just keep their mouths shut.

Remain open to even the most outrageous — or most ridiculous — ideas. An offbeat remark might end up triggering a suggestion from someone else, so instead of saying "good idea" or "I don' t think that will work" - try saying "thank you" when someone offers an idea, and move on to the next person.

Step 6 – Hire for the Heart

Encourage Collaboration

Focus on quantity, not quality, with comments like, "Wow, we've got 40 ideas. Let's see if we can get to 50."

You can feel the momentum of the team wax and wane as they warm up and slow down or get fatigued. So, if you only get 20 ideas, and you feel the energy start to lag – stop.

Evaluate Later

Postpone any criticism or weeding out of ideas to the end of the session (or even to a later meeting). Because evaluating ideas and generating ideas are two different brain functions, people can't easily switch between the two. In other words, creative thinking ability shuts down the minute you start analyzing.

The 11% Solution

Multivote

Multi-voting is a great way to quickly engage all participants and immediately see the preferences of the group as a whole.

A multi-vote is where each group member is given three or more votes to be allocated among several alternatives on your brainstormed list.

For instance, after identifying several standards of service, and writing them all on the flip chart, each group member might be given three small sticker-dots (votes) and told, "put your sticker-dots on your three favorite ideas."

After everyone puts stickers next to their "top three", the whole group can step back and see how the votes are distributed amongst all the ideas they've generated.

Now, it's easy to see what the group feels are the priority ideas, and no one gets their feelings hurt if their suggestion isn't picked.

You already know that I like to say "What does it look like?" So, I offer this diagram, which was helpful to me in further understanding the process.

Step 6 – Hire for the Heart

The Multivote Process

What	This strategy is a collaborative process used to select the most important items.
Why	This strategy is used when there is a variety of issues and opinions - and when group consensus is required.
How	1. Create a list of ideas as a whole group. 2. Record the list for everyone to see (eliminating duplicates) on a white board, blackboard, flip chart, etc 3. Provide individuals with sticky dots. (1 to 3 dots per person is usual.) 4. Each individual uses their dots to select the items they consider important. All dots can be placed on one item or spread across a number of items. (see the ideas generated under the "Fitness" example below) **FITNESS** weight training ☺ ☺ ☺ ☺ ☺ ☺ running ☺ ☺ ☺ ☺ aerobics ☺ ☺ ☺ cricket ☺ dancing ☺ ☺ ☺ fencing ☺ ☺ ☺ ☺ ☺ elbow bending ☺ ☺ ☺ ☺ ☺ ☺ ☺ ☺ ☺ ☺ 5. You can visually see the priority areas, in the example it is clearly "elbow bending".

Figure 5.0 – Multivote Process

The 11% Solution

Type up the flip chart favorites and re-present them to staff for a final "go-round", just to make sure the language is satisfactory to everyone. Then, make a poster of the final product.

Congrats! You've just built your first set
of Service Standards.

It's time to celebrate!

Signing party

This is really, really important. This whole process has been a big deal, but people won't take it seriously if you don't pursue it to the nth degree.

The next step is to recognize your staff's accomplishments in building the Service Standards. Bring some treats and invite all the head honchos (if you have them) to a signing party.

Each person on your staff uses a Sharpie to sign the Service Standards poster while enjoying a nosh. (Betty Crocker makes some wicked brownies, or can you say ice cream social?– m.m.m.m.. . .).

Step 6 – Hire for the Heart

Post standards

Your Service Standards becomes an important document both internally and externally.

Post the Service Standards where your customers can see them, and your staff can be proud of them. This signals to everyone that you expect the best, and tells your customers that you and your staff are passionate about making them happy.

Internally, keep a signed 8.5 x 11 version of the signed Service Standards in each staff person's personnel folder, and know that it's there to reference if you ever need to remind them of their commitment. This is a great coaching tool.

Earlier I commented on Leadership, and how one of the behaviors is setting expectations. Well, you've also just accomplished that – big time!

Hang in there - you're almost done. . . .

Role Play

So, now you've got your Service Standards, and the staff is loosening up. But, when you announce that you're going to hire a new person, staff may silently say to themselves, "uh oh, somebody new to upset the apple cart."

The 11% Solution

So, to alleviate everyone's stress, get them prepared for what's ahead, and inject some humor into the process, try role-playing with the staff.

Ask for a volunteer to be a customer – preferably a "cranky" customer. And then put that person back-to-back (like they're on a phone call) with a staff person who volunteers to be the agent.

The customer has license to act as outrageous as they can be, but the "agent" must employ all the customer service philosophies and strategies outlined in your newly posted Service Standards. (Maybe ask them to demonstrate a particular strategy that you've recently implemented, like "Service Recovery" – read step 3 – how to "Make It Right.")

This process can be a lot of fun – and really loosen everyone up for the interview phase.

Have a flip chart and marker available, or an erase board – somewhere that you can record their comments – and then just open it up for discussion. Here are some sample questions to guide your discussion.

What did you see?

What did you like?

What are some techniques that we can work on?

What qualities would you like in a future team mate?

Step 6 – Hire for the Heart

Because they just finished building their Service Standards, they're going to have some pretty solid ideas of what they want to see in a new hire. (Building Service Standards was some serious work, so I'm sure they don't want to hire "just anybody.")

Let me introduce you to more fun. . .

Below is a step-by-step variation on the same role play scenario and sure to give everybody a good laugh:

(1) Request someone to volunteer to be the **interviewer** and another person to be the **applicant**

(2) Take the applicant aside, and secretly give them a couple of behaviors to role play (see the "Applicant Q-cards" below)

(3) Give the interviewer a set of BBQ's – (see the "Behavioral-Based Questions" below)

(4) Turn them loose to conduct a mock interview. (Remember, the "interviewer" must remain professional at all times and ask "behavioral-based" questions.

(5) Let the group vote on who was the best "interviewer" and who was the best "applicant".

(6) Then recognize their efforts by ceremoniously presenting them with a bottle of BBQ Sauce and a medal.

(7) All joking aside –debrief the group by asking these questions:

What were some samples of BBQ's that were asked?

What behavior did the applicant demonstrate?

How did the interviewer handle it?

(I know, it may sound "cheezy", but I've done this with a group of executives, and it really is a lot of fun!

Behavioral – Based Questions

(BBQ's)

So what are BBQs?

Generally, they are open-ended questions (can't be answered by yes/no) that focus on how the applicant has responded to real work situations in the past.

Step 6 – Hire for the Heart

Ask for examples from past jobs rather than rely on answers about how they would behave in a hypothetical situation.

BBQs often center on such themes as teamwork, service attitude, taking initiative, communication and integrity.

See below for
5 of the Best Starters...

"Give me an example. . . "
Give me an example of how you keep track of your personal finances?

"Describe a time. . . "
Describe a time when you had a conflict with a co-worker?

"How have you demonstrated. . . "
How have you demonstrated that you are a valuable employee?

"What specific steps would you take. . ."
What specific steps would you take to resolve a customer complaint?

"Tell me about a time. . ."
Tell me about a time when you could have done better.

Applicant Q- Cards

In your interview...

be very, very
NERVOUS

- Fidget with your hair
- Pump your leg/foot
- Sort through your purse
- Don't make eye contact
- Chew gum
- Look at your watch

In your interview...

be *UNABLE TO COME UP WITH THE ANSWERS*

- Say "um" a lot
- Look confused – worried
- wrinkle your brow
- Can't think of examples
- Give one-word answers

In your interview...

be LATE

- Apologize profusely
- State that you're always running late
- Keep checking your watch
- State that you do great work, but are usually behind schedule

In your interview...

be DISRUPTIVE

- Play with items on the desk
- Laugh too loudly
- Wave & holler to people you know
- Walk away to introduce yourself to the team

In your interview… **provide INAPPROPRIATE ANSWERS** • Talk about personal issues • Exaggerate your experiences • Talk about your date • Offer "the boss" gum or cigarettes	In your interview… **be DEMANDING** • Focus on pay/benefits • State your preferred working conditions strongly • Ask: "What kind of a "boss" are you?" • Tell the interviewer how you like to dress on the job
In your interview… **DON'T MAKE EYE CONTACT** • Look at the floor/wall/desk	In your interview… **give ONE-WORD ANSWERS** • Don't offer supporting details • Make the interviewers probe for adequate responses

Figure 6.0 – Applicant Q-Cards

The 11% Solution

② Posting Process

OK, so now that you're all warmed up, let's move to Step 2

Include Service Language in All Communications – again it's about setting expectations. When you bombard an applicant with Service, Service, Service, they get the idea. Service is really important to you.

And another Leadership behavior is realized – you are clearly passionate about Service!

When an applicant is scanning the job postings, and they see the emphasis your job places on service, they'll make a note. But, won't they be surprised when they hear it emphasized in every step of the recruiting and hiring process!

As a result, they will either commit, or "deselect", depending on whether they feel they're up to the task of providing the level of service you and your team are expecting.

And, I don't have to tell you, you should be so lucky if someone "de-selects" and doesn't pursue your opening.

Seriously, you want to avoid anyone who doesn't feel that they can treat your customers with the care and concern you expect.

Step 6 – Hire for the Heart

Below is an example of a job posting that emphasizes "service" language.

Job Title	Service Representative
Reports To	Manager
Date	2010

POSITION PURPOSE   (Service Language in *italics*)

Answers incoming calls on customer line. *Team members in this department are expected to provide customers with high quality customer service - both on the telephone and face to face. Team members in this department are expected to demonstrate a "can-do" attitude, and partner with co-workers and management to exceed customer expectations. (see Service Standards)*

ESSENTIAL DUTIES & RESPONSIBILITIES

➢ Answers phone calls in 3 rings or less.
➢ Announces name, company, and "How can I help you?"
➢ Promotes customer satisfaction by providing timely resolution of problems. Uses service strategies to handle complaints and problems in such a way as to diffuse anger and frustration - improving the customer's perception of service.
➢ Records all phone calls (complaints, concerns, inquiries) in customer contact database.
➢ Reports trends at weekly staff meeting.
➢ Recommends action to respond to trends.
➢ Works with others to implement changes.

The 11% Solution

JOB SPECIFICATIONS

- ➤ 5+ years in customer service environment.
- ➤ Relevant Bachelor's degree preferred.
- ➤ Demonstrated ability to answer the phone and communicate well with customers.
- ➤ Demonstrated ability to provide service recovery strategies to turn unhappy customers into loyal customers.
- ➤ Demonstrated ability to identify trends.

Figure 7.0 –Job Posting with Service Language

This is easy – but, it's simply the first pass.

When you make that initial phone call to invite the applicant in for an interview, pay special attention. Even if they are on their best behavior, you will get an idea of their phone skills, tone of voice, etc.

Step 6 – Hire for the Heart

Know the Stats!
Call references!
Establish the Track Record!

. . . . Because, it's the best predictor of future performance.

Share your newly established Service Standards with the applicant. Discuss your expectations regarding Service, how you expect the customers (and team mates) to be treated, and the consequences of not doing so.

Ask the applicant to read over the Service Standards and pick the one that has the most meaning to them. Then discuss it.

If the applicant seems like they might be a good fit with your operations, invite them to continue with the panel interview.

You're on the home stretch, and well on your way to finding that perfect person.

The final leg of this relay is to conduct a panel interview.

131

The 11% Solution

Before we delve in the panel interview process, I'd like you to read these articles. Two of the best links I've ever read on interviewing technique and questions are:

"Dig Deeper":

Tuesday, December 23, 2008 7:00 AM by Steve Bruce

http://hrdailyadvisor.blr.com/archive/2008/12/23/Hiring_and_Recruiting_Asking_Effective_Interviewing_Questions_Probe_Probing.aspx

"Why It Pays To Give a Damn?":

Friday, 14 May 2010 | 11:56 AM ET

By: Gloria McDonough-Taub CNBC, Senior Editor, Blogs

www.cnbc.com/id/37149447/

Now, back to the panel interview, which revolves around the use of a "Red Flag" document. The Red Flag document is designed to do four things:

Step 6 – Hire for the Heart

(1) Get everyone involved

The more you can involve your current employees – the more they will be willing to help train and support the new hire. Peer Pressure can undermine your new hire lickety-split, and it can be mitigated by getting all staff involved.

Based on your Service Standards, previous role-play exercises, and the articles above, the staff will have suggestions for questions that they'd like to ask an applicant.

Your role is to help them craft their ideas into "behavioral-based" questions – and then identify the "red flag" response to watch out for.

(2) Set the right expectations

So you're passionate about service? To quote Captain Ron, "It shows." Now's a good time to let everyone know just what you expect from your employees – present & future!

Also, when you spend this kind of quality time "up front', you're sending a powerful message that you care a great deal about finding the right "fit" for your team.

The 11% Solution

(3) Ensure that you ask everyone the same questions

This sets a great example for your staff and demonstrates to them that you treat everyone fairly.

(4) Identify potential problems ("red flags")

"Red Flags" are warning signs. If you think you might have a "red flag" response, ask probing questions to get to the bottom of the issue.

If the applicant can't alleviate your concerns, or shows signs of uncertainty or confusion – they may not fit well with the team, and certainly not with your customers!

You can use any kind of a grid you want to capture questions and responses. Just make sure it's the same for each applicant. At the end of each applicant interview, score the questions.

Again, don't re-invent the wheel. Make it easy on yourself (and the staff). Review the links to the articles listed to give you and the staff some ideas for interview questions. To give you an example, two of my favorite questions & subsequent "red flag" responses are:

Step 6 – Hire for the Heart

Q: What are you most proud of?

A: Licking my elbow = Red Flag

Q: Anything you're not proud of?

A: No, nothing = Red flag.

Other Red flags:

- Applicant's questions are focused on benefits
- Job-hopping is detected on the application or resume
- Typos in resumes, etc.
- Applicant handles problems with co-workers by "taking it to the supervisor"

Let me give you a more comprehensive example of what a "Red Flag" document might looks like. The following was built by one of my clients, after they had completed the process of building Service Standards. Before the applicant arrived, they assigned one question to each person on the panel interview team.

The 11% Solution

Questions	"Gold Stars"	"Red Flags"	Score
What is your Customer Service experience?	Able to identify customers	Cannot answer	None Avg. Exc. 1 2 3 4 5 Comments:
What companies have you worked at that required Customer Service experience?	Every company requires some type of customer service experience	Does not recall having customer service experience	None Avg. Exc. 1 2 3 4 5 Comments:
Would you work for those companies again in the future (Why/why not?)	Praises past employers	Speaks negatively of past employers	None Avg. Exc. 1 2 3 4 5 Comments:
Who will be your customers at ABC Company?	Identify staff (internal) & patrons (external)	People who come into the store	None Avg. Exc. 1 2 3 4 5 Comments:
What do you do to create a positive first impression with a customer?	Smile; eye contact; introduce self & explain role	Crack a joke	None Avg. Exc. 1 2 3 4 5 Comments:

Figure 8.0 – Red Flag Document

Take it to the front lines.

Some experts estimate that as much as 95% of your company's reputation with customers (and potential customers) results from the performance of your frontline, customer-facing staff.

This "Hiring for the Heart" is serious stuff, no matter if you're filling an entry level or highly skilled position. So maximize "word of mouth". Always refer to the "5 Easy Steps" document when searching for the person that demonstrates the right blend of technical and service expertise. And, as a quick summary to assist you with "Hiring for the Heart", remember these important tips:

- *Dialogue with staff regarding the service behaviors and qualities you are looking for in a candidate*

- *Involve staff to conduct a panel interview of the top candidate*

- *During the interview, communicate your department's Service Standards*

- *Ask Behavior-based Interview Questions to tease out past service performance*

STEP 7

Protect Your Investment

*"From what we get, we can make a living;
what we give, however, makes a life."*

Arthur Ashe, late tennis star

Sure your employees owe you their loyalty.
However, they won't give it to you unless you earn it.

The 11% Solution

And to that end, too many small businesses overlook the importance of education in creating the kind of employee that really wants to stay on the job, give it their all, and take care in handling your customers.

It isn't just me that says this. To quote an article published by Survey Methods in 2006:

"Too many businesses think education is overly expensive and only for big corporations

Teach them (your employees) how to engage, talk to (your clients), and turn them into loyal customers."

www.surveymethods.com/glossary/article_customer_service_seg_l.aspx

Sounds good, but you may need more than one survey quote to convince you that taking valuable time away from your production schedule to provide additional education and training is going to ultimately grow your business. So here's another set of experts weighing in on the subject:

Dr. Beverly Kaye is an internationally recognized authority on career issues, employee engagement and retention in the workplace. She is the Founder and CEO of Career Systems International (CSi) and a best-selling author on workplace performance. Sharon Jordan-Evans,

Step 7 – Protect Your Investment

president of the Jordan Evans Group, is a pioneer in the field of employee retention and engagement.

Together, they asked over 3,000 people why they stayed with an organization. The top 7 reasons are:

1. Career growth, learning & development
2. Exciting & challenging work
3. Meaningful work – making a difference and a contribution
4. Great people
5. Being part of a team
6. Good boss
7. Recognition

Let's devote some time to the #1 reason – Career growth; learning & development. I'm going to take liberties with this category and translate it into Orientation and Training, or "protecting your investment."

And, as you read on, you'll see that I interchange the words "orientation", "training" and "education." That's because whatever you call it, it's all related to gaining knowledge. Providing educational opportunities for the staff to learn and grow also reinforces the process of bonding between Leader and staff.

Everybody struggles with the age-old quandary, "there's too much work to do already, and we'll just get further behind if we have to do training or try different processes!"

The 11% Solution

But, here's the thing, education (training) doesn't have to cost you an arm & a leg or delay your production schedule.

I was at a recent economic development conference for the eighth largest economy in the world (California!), and I quote from the advisory panel of seasoned business men and women who have operated in up and down environments for 20 years or more:

> "It's much more cost effective to train internally, and in the long run, your workforce will be MORE productive.

And, internal or "in-house" training can be just as satisfying for your employees.

So, regardless of whether you have the budget to send someone "outside" for training, or if you're providing training "in-house", it (training) begins immediately after you hire - and it all starts in the workplace.

For example, many employers provide their new hires with an orientation: show them where the bathrooms are, tell them when to take breaks and lunches, and then turn them over to the most senior staff to "show them the ropes."

This is a good start, but it isn't enough. There's nothing that will make a new employee more disgruntled or dissatisfied with their workplace than lack of

Step 7 – Protect Your Investment

orientation and training – and attention from the "leader" that hired them.

Without the proper attention to their knowledge needs, you're very likely to end up with low morale and an unproductive work force. This, in turn, will be felt by your customers.

Bottom line, we're in this to make money, and if your employees are disgruntled, they're unproductive and won't care about your customers. That hurts business.

Now, I don't think anyone goes around with the intention of burning out or "churning" employees. But, if you're less than vigilant about this education thing, and lackadaisical about the career growth of even the most entry level position, you may be fostering a less than welcoming environment.

So, how do you create employees who stay and feel valued?

We've already established that you don't have the budget to send someone outside for a class. (You may have convinced yourself, that it's *just* an entry level job– and you've decided that you're not going to spend any more money on a frontline employee that's probably going to leave in a couple of months, anyway.)

And, I understand that thinking, to an extent. But, (I hope) you've already devoted a considerable amount of everyone's time and energy in finding the right person for the job, so now's not the time to slack off. Protect that investment, and reduce the overall costs of doing

The 11% Solution

business, by creating employees who feel valued and want to work for YOU.

There is a path to providing education that grows your business, and it's very similar to recognition, in that it must be "meaningful." Don't be in a rush. Resist sending someone to a seminar or training event "just because" it's on your list, or it's the "right thing to do." Wait if you have to, and find the right type of education that matters to both you and the employee. Otherwise, you're very likely to throw good money after bad.

Leaders understand the importance of providing employees with opportunities to grow personally and professionally. So, observe the employee's performance. Give them feedback on areas of opportunity and success. Identify their interests, as well as those that will help your business prosper. Then, provide them with training and education that supports your business and also meets their personal goal. Make Your Buck Go Bang!

Besides developing and communicating the career progression to the employee, I've listed some additional "no cost/low cost" incentives other than salary:

- Work from home
- 4-day work week
- Titles
- Cross-training
- Opportunities for advancement
- Career Ladder
- Recognition for attaining a goal
- Business Cards

Step 7 – Protect Your Investment

Yes, business cards. This can be a great incentive. For example, I met with a group of employees working to improve customer satisfaction, and they wanted nothing more than to have a business card - with a blank for their name - that they could hand to customers. The manager said, "No."

Are you kidding me? "No?" Here I am asking employees to do more with less and improve customer satisfaction to boot, and all they want is a generic business card?

They didn't want fancy seminars, or "boot camps" – all they wanted was a business card. And, if that's all it takes to make them happy and keep morale high - I'm going to buy a box of business cards. Wouldn't you?

But, if the manager says "no", I need to respect that decision. However, it *was just* a box of generic business cards, and I was struggling with understanding the decision (surely, I wasn't aware of some sinister underlying issue that wasn't obvious to me at the moment.)

Giving the manager the benefit of the doubt, I suggested (in private) that we "pilot" the process. Buy one box of business cards (e.g., Vista Print is currently offering 500 cards for $10.00), and see how it goes before making a bigger investment.

It was then that I realized the root of this organization's customer service problem, because the manager actually told me "no", again, to my face.

The 11% Solution

He didn't want the employees to "run around" giving out their names, along with the company contact information to customers, because he was afraid customers would call.!!!!

This was before the prevalence of the internet where customer contact information is on every website. But, still, I couldn't believe what I was hearing. No wonder this staff felt disgruntled, unhappy, and customer satisfaction was suffering.

The manager continued to have a high department turnover rate, and they never did get their business cards. (I always felt bad about that.) But, I digress. . .

Another very valuable "no cost" thing you can do when it comes to training is develop a career ladder. No matter what the level of job duties, design a next level. Then, let your employee know exactly what they need to do to move up that level.

Back to the "meaningful" issue - whatever type of training you pick, whether it's internal or provided by an outside company, always make it clear to the employee that you will follow-up with them when they return to work.

In fact, set the follow-up appointment before they ever leave for the training so they know you're not kidding. Then, make sure to actually hold the meeting!

Follow-through and accountability– leadership behaviors! (Plus, there's no way I'm going to send someone to training and not have it "pay off" for my business.)

Step 7 – Protect Your Investment

In the follow-up meeting, the employee will be expected to tell me what they learned and relate it to their job goals. (Plus, the employees will just enjoy spending time with you and discussing their experience – any time spent with you on-on-one is a form of recognition.)

And, speaking of goals, I cannot believe that of all the clients I have worked with, maybe one has actually set a goal for their employees. And, you know why that is. .?

Because, if you set a goal, you have to meet regularly with the employee to touch base on their progress. This takes time. But it's all an integral part of behaving like a leader.

I could go on and on about the importance of education in protecting your investment, but you get the idea. Besides, I promised that you could get through a step in 15 minutes, and I think I'm running out of time.

Really quickly, let me show you some tools that were developed by my clients for observing performance. This particular client was a doctor's office that wanted to improve the performance of their receptionists:

The 11% Solution

WORKPLACE OBSERVATION ASSESSMENT TOOL

NAME: _____ DATE: _____

DEPT: _____ OBSERVER: _____

INSTRUCTION: Rate the employee on a scale from 1 to 5.
If the item is not applicable, use N/A instead of a number.
(1 = never, 2 = seldom, 3= occasionally, 4 = often, 5 = always)

A.	GREETS CUSTOMERS	
		core
1.	Greets customer with a smile and/or a positive tone of voice.	
2.	Acknowledges customer's presence quickly, even if busy with work (face-to-face only).	
3.	Uses customer's name at first opportunity	
4.	Demonstrates full attention and listens actively to what the customer is saying by commenting on what the customer says (not just "uh-huh" or "that's nice").	
5.	Uses polite words, e.g. "please", "excuse me", and "thank you".	

B.	LISTENS AND DETERMINES PATIENT'S/CUSTOMER'S CONCERNS	
6.	If patient/customer thinks organization has made a mistake, expresses concern, apologizes for the inconvenience, and takes personal responsibility for correcting it.	
7.	When a customer is upset, helps sort out the situation and assures the customer that he/she will personally help resolve it.	
8.	Remains calm and receptive when customer is critical of the representative/employee or the product.	

C.	HANDLES SITUATIONS	
9.	Handles situations personally whenever possible so the supervisor does not have to become involved causing delay and customer feeling "passed around".	

Step 7 – Protect Your Investment

10.	When you can't solve the customer's problem, takes initiative to assure that the customer is helped (uses "warm" handoff).	
11.	Doesn't quote policy to the customer.	
12.	Provides service guarantee to the customer.	
13.	When service is delayed, apologizes and informs patient/customer about the delay.	
14.	Does not conduct personal conversations in front of the customer.	

D.	CLOSES INTERACTIONS	
15.	Asks the customer: "What can I do to assist you further today?"	
16.	Thanks the customer for the business.	

Figure 9.0 – Workplace Observation Tool

This is a pretty good form, and I recommend you take 5 minutes of your time to use it. The majority of the work is done for you. You just have to figure out how to make it work for your situation.

So, find a clipboard, attach this form, and observe any of your staff who is interacting with one of your customers. Make a few tweaks to make it match your situation, and conform to some of your recent teachings.

Are they utilizing some of the customer service tips and techniques that you've been discussing lately?

They'd better be – but if they're not, that's exactly what this form is for. This moment of observation is crucial. If the staff get no sense that you're going to hold them accountable for their actions, they'll just revert to

The 11% Solution

whatever they've been doing that's worked for them in the past.

But, be prepared for what you see. Just remember, stay in the coaching mode, and tell yourself over and over that behaviors don't change overnight. Continue to observe and give feedback, observe and give feedback, observe and give feedback.

This method will alleviate any concerns that this observation tool will be used for anything other than coaching. (Some staff may feel you're using an observation form to catch them doing something wrong – and a form of punishment will ensue). If you do this, staff will cooperate and start to change behavior.

However, if you do nothing, and all of a sudden, the employee is called to your office to receive "counseling", the entire staff will quickly start to associate observation with consequences, and that's not good.

Use observation to support your employee and keep telling them that everything you do is intended to HELP them reach their goal and receive a good evaluation.

Oh no, not evaluations!

Oh yes. I don't care what it looks like. It can be a sticky note placed in their file. Just remember that the evaluation needs to be linked to a goal. And, you need to discuss the goal every couple of months to make sure the employee is "on track." Link the goal language to your recent observations - and ultimately, to the employee's salary.

There can absolutely be no surprises here. If all of a sudden, a "need for improvement" shows up on an employee's yearly evaluation, and they weren't expecting it – well, that can "take down" even the best employee, and don't think it will be kept private. The employee will talk, and eventually, the entire staff will hear the employee's version of your behavior.

But, that's not what you want. You want everyone to act consistently with your customers, and utilize the customer service strategies and techniques that you know will make a difference to your company's bottom line. Plus, you want to be a great leader!

So, that's about it. Just remember that education includes any kind of knowledge transfer – it can be as formal as a class, or as simple as a departmental orientation - it all counts.

And, the frosting on the cake is "observation & feedback." Then the whole cycle starts all over again – i.e., training, observation, feedback – training observation, feedback.

Don't throw good money after bad!

"Protect Your Investment"

I look forward to chatting with you, soon.

More FACTOIDS

According to Adam Urbanski, a marketing guru, 80% of all sales are made after the prospect has heard from you at least seven times. Yet a typical business owner gives up after one or two times.

Eric Fraterman is a customer service consultant who re-states a statistic from Price Waterhouse Cooper's *Trendsetter Barometer*, "Over the past five years, on average, companies planning customer service initiatives have increased their revenues 46% faster than their peers."

From *The Loyalty Effect* by Frederick Reichheld, "Reducing customer defection by 5% could increase profitability by 25% – 80%."

In a report by *Forum*, a leader in the field of workplace learning, "65% of customers switched providers because they were not being treated courteously."

Michael Hepworth, author of *The Street Smart Marketer,* is quoted in a Canadian Marketing Assoc. publication as saying:

"$1 spent on advertising yields less than $5 in incremental growth, yet $1 spent on customer service yields $60 in incremental growth."

The 11% Solution

Only 1 in 3 customers who contact an organization for help are satisfied with the response they get.

A recent Bain & Company survey of 362 firms found that 80% believed they delivered a "superior" customer service experience. The customers of those firms gave them a rating of 8%.

Summary

Make Your Buck Go Bang

If you implement just one of the "7 Steps to Make Your Buck Go Bang," I guarantee, your business will grow through "word of mouth" advertising. So keep up the good fight, don't throw away your money, and remember you can start to do something about that 11% immediately!

Don't forget to visit the blog and leave a comment at www.theSERVICEadvisors.com/blog.

Thank you for taking the time to read the "11% Solution", and know that I'm just a contact away. Visit my website at www.theserviceadvisors.com, and tell me about your situation. I'd love to help you Make Your Buck Go Bang!

Looking forward to hearing back from you, and wishing you much success,

V

Resources

1.   The Service Advisors Hotline

1-888-822-1253

2.   The Service Advisors website:
www.theserviceadvisors.com

3.   The Service Advisors Blog
www.theserviceadvisors.com/blog

4.   Link to Graphs, Figures and Articles

www.theserviceadvisors.com/7stepresources.html